cooking in the moment

cooking
IN THE
moment

A Year of Seasonal Recipes

ANDREA REUSING

CLARKSON POTTER/PUBLISHERS

New York

All rights reserved.
Published in the United States by Clarkson Potter/Publishers
an imprint of the Crown Publishing Group, a division of
Random House, Inc., New York.
www.crownpublishing.com
www.clarksonpotter.com

CLARKSON POTTER is a trademark and POTTER with
colophon is a registered trademark of Random House, Inc.

Library of Congress Cataloging-in-Publication Data

Reusing, Andrea.
  Cooking in the moment / Andrea Reusing. — 1st ed.
      p. cm.
  Includes index.
  1. Cookery (Natural foods). 2. Menus. I. Title.

TX741.R49 2010
641.5'636—dc22   2010018532

ISBN 978-0-307-46389-0

Printed in China

Book design by Marysarah Quinn
Jacket photographs by John Kernick

10 9 8 7 6 5 4 3 2 1

FIRST EDITION

For Mac, Oona, and Arthur

contents

introduction 8

spring 13 summer 65

fall 145   winter 207

sources 264

acknowledgments 267

index 268

INTRODUCTION

At work, I am a cook first, but in the rest of my life I am an eater. My strongest childhood memories involve food: going to Chinatown in Manhattan for Peking duck before a Yankees game, eating smoky Lebanon baloney at Lancaster's Central Market, hearing the rousing anthem our mom still sings as she reveals a surprise box of ice cream sandwiches after dinner. One of my earliest recollections is of my grandmother Marie taking a pot pie big enough to feed twenty-five people out of her oven and resting it on the open oven door for a moment while she grabbed another mitt. It slid off the door and flipped neatly onto the floor. Following my cousin Terry's lead, we took turns kneeling down next to the heap of steaming pie and served ourselves a plate, the desire to comfort Marie nearly as great as our hunger for her pot pie. Food is love, and while dieticians warn us not to confuse the two, how can we help it?

Arriving home for lunch one day from grade school a few minutes before my mom, I ran to the house next door, complaining of extreme, possibly dangerous hunger. Mrs. Galliers got out a big cast-iron skillet and made grilled cheese sandwiches of the old school, with four neat pats of butter (on each side), and then sent me back across the driveway with a tin of pecan sandies. Every day after that, I ran home from school, hoping to slip past my mom so I could ring the Galliers' doorbell for further introduction to flavors never before seen in our whole-wheat household: soft Bibb lettuce with green goddess dressing, rare prime rib, and fresh coconut cake. I still think about the chocolate cream pie Mrs. Galliers served my brother, Tim, and me for dessert when we slept over at their house the night our brother Brendan was born.

Always hungry, eventually I had to learn to feed myself. The first things I tried cooking when I left home were the dishes I grew up with: my mom's scalloped potatoes and ham, the fried rice my parents made together from Virginia Lee and Craig Claiborne's *Chinese Cookbook*, Marie's apple dumplings with cold heavy cream. Most of the friendships

I made as a new adult happened around my wobbly dinner table or in restaurants tasting pierogies and kimchi for the first time.

When I left New York for North Carolina in 1996, I worried about the adjustment to living in a small Southern town. The not-quite-a-joke among friends was that my biggest challenge would be leaving the grocery stores and restaurants of the city; they'd imagine me losing my mind in the produce aisle when told that there was no Swiss chard.

It's true that I wasn't ready for my new life. In the beginning, I didn't get that the word *yankee* could be more descriptive than pejorative. I honked my horn. Twenty-seven years old, I shuddered when called "ma'am" and couldn't sit through a basketball game. In line at the hardware store, I grumbled waiting through the inevitable good-byes. During a plumbing disaster at our rural farmhouse, I learned where (and what) the septic tank was.

It turns out I was as clueless about food as I had been about plumbing. The Carrboro farmers' market, opened in 1978, was flourishing. There, I could buy German Johnson and Cherokee Purple tomatoes with more personality than any variety I had ever eaten growing up in New Jersey, field peas, fresh goat cheese from Celebrity Dairy, and yes,

Swiss chard. Within just a few years, farms here were selling chickens that had been raised outdoors, heritage pork that had been bred for flavor, milk and cheese from grass-fed cows. The selection at my old seafood market had seemed exhaustive, but at Tom Robinson's seafood market I could get meaty black drum; porgies; enlightening versions of favorites like squid, tiny and still in their sparkling purple skins; and soft-shell crabs that had been swimming the night before. Butcher Cliff Collins, in business since 1973, cured his own bacon and was willing to teach me the fundamentals of hog butchery whenever I showed up at his back door with a whole pig. *Tiendas* and *tacquerias* were opening, bringing life to formerly foodless blocks with fresh produce and homemade tortillas. At the coffee shop, you could overhear two medical students ignoring their studies to discuss crop rotation. I had moved to a place where the most coveted seat for dinner was not at a restaurant, but at a farmer's potluck.

Living here, eating food from close to home—at friends' tables, in restaurants, and in my own kitchen—clarified the idea that most delicious and memorable things to eat are real foods: fresh farm eggs, soft-boiled on toast; pan-roasted clams, just out of the water; a perfect, ripe tomato, sprinkled with salt. Cooking became less about what flavors I could scheme to combine or track down and more about what was already here.

Before moving south, I would have viewed a mostly local diet as a limitation; but when I started to reimagine seasonality as a shopping list, the result was freeing. I think of "cooking in the moment" as focusing on one meal at a time—an icy, spicy cucumber soup on an August night, a glass of tangerine juice on a frosty morning, or soft, braised shortribs with horseradish on a gray fall day. Cooking and eating in the moment allows food in season to become a reason for celebration—a Friday-night dinner made entirely from the first CSA share in spring; a whole week of fresh-picked corn every day; a blue-moon autumn asparagus harvest; a rich stew made with the last few sweet potatoes of winter.

This book is a year of cooking from spring through winter for friends and family at home using mostly ingredients from nearby. Many of the recipes included here are impromptu, some are from friends, and one is cribbed from Girl Scout camp. The recipes are a mix of

childhood favorites, standbys that can be prepared quickly, simple restaurant dishes, and celebration dishes to feed a crowd. Some are so simple that they don't really qualify as recipes, and that is the point. While I couldn't ignore some regional treats (like ramps, figs, and wild shrimp), most of the ingredients used in the recipes are basics available nearly everywhere, when in season. And while the action takes place here in North Carolina, the kinds of producers and artisans featured—farmers, ranchers, cheese makers, fishmongers, butchers, and bakers—work and live almost everywhere, producing the flavors that we crave.

spring

BROCCOLI AND CAULIFLOWER PAGE 16
    Cauliflower Gratin with Aged Raw Milk Cheese
    Grilled Broccoli with Parsley, Garlic, and Anchovies

FRESH OSSABAW HAM PAGE 20
    Roast Fresh Ham with Cracklings
    Carrot Soup with Toasted Curry and Pistachios

SPRING MOUNTAIN PAGE 25
    Cast-Iron-Skillet Fresh Trout with Cornmeal
    Wilted Ramps
    Campfire Bacon and Eggs in a Bag

WILD SHRIMP PAGE 30
    Shrimp, Pea, and Rice Stew

ASPARAGUS FEAST PAGE 32
    Asparagus with Butter and Soy
    Charcoal-Grilled Asparagus

OUTDOOR BIRDS PAGE 36
  Hen and Dumplings
  Raw Vegetables with Garlic-Anchovy Mayonnaise

MILK MONEY PAGE 41
  Warm Fresh Mozzarella with Grits, Grilled Radicchio,
    and Balsamic

LOG-GROWN MUSHROOMS PAGE 46
  Roasted Shiitake Mushrooms with Garlic Oil
  Pea Greens with Ume Plum Vinaigrette and Chive Blossoms
  Rhubarb-Ginger Sorbet

KID-CHURNED ICE CREAM PAGE 51
  Strawberry Ice Cream
  Fresh Peas with Lettuce and Green Garlic

SEAFOOD MARKET PAGE 54
  Grilled Spanish Mackerel with Green Sauce
  Potato Salad
  Crispy Pan-Fried Catfish with Hot Slaw
  Pan-Roasted Clams with Sake
  Crab and Garlic Fried Rice

BROCCOLI AND CAULIFLOWER

This morning there is finally something stirring at the market. No one ever exclaims, "Honey, it's broccoli season!" but for a few months a year, in spring and again in the early fall, broccoli and cauliflower are so good and fresh that they command attention. Wrapped giftlike in pale leaves, the four small, creamy heads of cauliflower cost $10 but will be the foundation of several meals this week. Simmered in salted water with a splash of milk until just tender, then drained and mashed, cauliflower is a savory base for bay scallops from Harkers Island; served with wilted spinach, it's an in-law-worthy dinner in half an hour. Cut in large thin slices straight across the entire head, stem and all, then caramelized in a hot oven along with sliced apple and finished with pine nuts and wine-plumped golden raisins, cauliflower makes a savory-sweet dish that is great on its own with a warm wilted salad or as a side for roast pork shoulder. The same flexibility is found in gratineed cauliflower, which partners with dressed greens or serves as a side for a roast hen.

Today Cathy Jones of Perry-winkle Farm has small stalks of broccoli that are an intense jade green from flower to stem and are tender even raw. Friends are here for lunch and so I lightly grill the broccoli for a little smoke and then toss it with salty anchovies, parsley, and lemon zest. We sit down to eat with the broccoli piled on a big platter in the middle of the table, along with warm soft-boiled eggs and thick slices of grilled bread rubbed with raw garlic, and wash it all down with a slightly bubbly rosé. For dessert, some overripe mandarin oranges and Annie's pistachio macarons from the coffee shop.

cauliflower gratin with aged raw milk cheese

SERVES 4 TO 6 AS A SIDE OR 2 AS A MAIN DISH

Kosher salt
2 small heads of cauliflower
2 large eggs
1 cup heavy cream
Freshly grated nutmeg
1½ cups grated aged raw milk cheese

Preheat the oven to 450°F. Bring a large pot of salted water to a boil.

Cut the cauliflower heads in half with a sharp knife. Remove the cores and any leaves. Cut the cauliflower into large florets. Cook the florets in the boiling water for about 3 minutes until just tender but still firm in the center. Drain and arrange the cauliflower in a 9 × 13 baking dish.

In a small bowl, whisk together the eggs, cream, a little salt, and nutmeg to taste. Pour over the warm cauliflower. Bake for 30 to 40 minutes until the gratin is just barely set in the center. Remove from the oven and turn on the broiler. Sprinkle the cauliflower with the cheese and broil for about 3 minutes until the top is golden brown.

grilled broccoli with parsley, garlic, and anchovies

Delicate fresh broccoli and cauliflower from a garden or small farm don't resemble the useful California sorts that are a fixture in our produce drawer the rest of the year, and so we enjoy them while we can. But because broccoli and cauliflower do travel and keep exceptionally well, I make these recipes year-round, just allowing for slightly longer cooking times when dealing with more mature vegetables.

SERVES 4

2 small bunches of tender broccoli
2 tablespoons olive oil, plus more for serving
6 anchovy fillets, minced
2 garlic cloves, mashed to a paste
Grated zest of 1 lemon
⅓ cup finely chopped fresh flat-leaf parsley leaves
2 teaspoons chile flakes, or to taste

Prepare a hot fire in a charcoal grill.

Cut the broccoli lengthwise to make long florets with all of the tender stem attached. Blanch in well-salted boiling water for just 15 to 20 seconds, a little longer if the broccoli is very mature. Drain well, transfer to a medium bowl, and toss with 1 tablespoon of the oil. When the flame has died down and the coals are completely covered with ash, grill the broccoli to slightly char it all over.

Mix the anchovies, garlic, lemon zest, parsley, remaining 1 tablespoon oil, and chile flakes in a bowl. Add the grilled broccoli, toss well, and serve with olive oil at the table for drizzling.

FRESH OSSABAW HAM

I drank a few cups of strong coffee outside on the patio this morning; it was almost strong enough to handle kids who have eaten nothing but chocolate and jelly beans since waking at 6:30 a.m. Silvia Pahola, my partner in the kitchen at Lantern, is here and we are cooking an Easter meal for about twenty friends. Her love of pork is unrivaled; in fact, if she ever writes a cookbook, she already knows its title: *Pork Is a Fruit: It Grows on Pigs*. To paraphrase the late novelist and food writer Laurie Colwin, Silvia is the best kind of friend to eat and cook with: someone who happily talks about what to have for lunch while still cooking breakfast. We both like to eat pork on Easter: she sometimes does ribs or roast shoulder, while I tend toward a fresh ham.

The ham in my oven now (so deliciously porky that a neighbor just rang the bell) was raised by another member of the pork-is-a-fruit school, Eliza MacLean of Cane Creek Farm, in Snow Camp (just outside of Chapel Hill). Pigs are joyful, emotional animals who take pleasure in almost everything they do, from rolling in the mud on a hot day to eating peanuts. Eliza's pigs may be the happiest anywhere, frolicking in the woods and meadows of the 500-acre farm, which she runs with Dr. Charles Sydnor, who raises grass-fed Red Devon cattle next door at Braeburn Farm. A mom with young twins, Eliza is also a pig farmer on a mission: to help reestablish the Ossabaw, a rare breed descended from the Ibérico or *pata negra* hog, those free-roaming pigs who fatten up on acorns and wild grasses before becoming arguably the best ham anywhere: *ibérico de bellota*. Brought to the American South in the sixteenth century by Spanish explorers, these hogs were stranded on Ossabaw, a barrier island off the coast of Savannah, Georgia; the hogs adapted to island life, developing the ability to store ample quantities of fat, which has a silky, buttery quality all its own. As lucky as we are to have Eliza and her pigs as neighbors, we have also had success with Easter ham using pork from many sources: Berkshire hogs mail-ordered from Heritage Foods USA; conventional pork sourced from Cliff's, our local meat market in Carrboro; and whey-fed pig from Chapel Hill Creamery.

Silvia carves the roast, which is finally out of the oven and done resting. The meat flips away from her knife into big, juicy slices—the amber crackling skin is the only condiment we need. It's a very good ham, but also a recipe for a happy afternoon: making lunch with food from a farm we love, talking about our next meal. What's left of the succulent meat will be thinly sliced for Cuban sandwiches tomorrow, and the bones will be the start of a pot of soup the following day.

roast fresh ham with cracklings

Silvia and I have made this often over the years, the first time in my (illegal) home kitchen for an Easter catering gig when we made the entire meal twice, timing it so that the second roast was perfectly blistered and crispy when we arrived back home with a car full of dirty pots and pans to have dinner with our own families. It goes well with wilted spring scallions, roast potatoes (basted in the drippings), lightly dressed spicy arugula, and beans in all forms. One favorite bean dish for this ham is from Amanda Hesser's *The Cook and the Gardener:* flavorful white beans simmered with hearty herbs and crème fraîche until slightly thickened.

SERVES 15 OR MORE, WITH LEFTOVERS

Kosher salt
2 heads of garlic, unpeeled, cut in half crosswise
1 large yellow onion, cut in half
1 tablespoon black peppercorns
1 tablespoon coriander seeds
3 dried bay leaves
1 small bunch of fresh flat-leaf parsley
1 tablespoon expeller-pressed vegetable oil
1 (15- to 18-pound) trimmed, skin-on fresh ham

Combine 4 quarts cold water, 1 cup salt, and the garlic, onion, peppercorns, coriander, bay leaves, and parsley in a container that is large enough to hold the ham, and stir until the salt is dissolved. Submerge the ham in the liquid and refrigerate for at least 24 hours and up to 3 days. (Alternatively, if you can't fit the ham in your refrigerator, brine it directly in a clean cooler, just adding a little extra salt and enough ice to keep the ham cold, draining a little brine and adding more ice as needed.)

Preheat the oven to 350°F.

Drain off the brine, discarding all the seasonings, and pat the ham dry. Put a paper towel on top of a cutting board and set the ham on top of that so that it doesn't slip. With a sharp knife, score the skin with incisions that run the length of the ham and are about ½ inch apart, and then again the other way to form a crosshatch pattern. The incisions should just barely reach into the fat under the skin; do not cut into the meat itself, in order to help the crackling skin stay in one piece once it is crispy. Allow the ham to come to room temperature.

RECIPE CONTINUES

Lightly oil and salt the meat, rubbing it in on all surfaces. Put the ham on a rack or on a few rolled-up sheets of aluminum foil in a large heavy roasting pan and put it in the oven. A 15-pound roast will take almost 4 hours total, while an 18-pounder will take as long as 5— about 15 minutes per pound. About 2½ hours in, when the temperature of the ham hits about 130°F, raise the oven temperature to 425°F to crisp the skin (cover any areas that start to get too dark with a piece of foil). When the meat thermometer reads 145° to 150°F, remove the roast and allow it to rest, loosely tented with foil, for an hour or so before carving.

carrot soup with toasted curry and pistachios

I love any dish that can be made using water rather than stock. It's a bit of useful laziness that can help establish the clean, pure flavor of the ingredient itself, whether it's carrots or clams. One key is a slow, patient approach to cooking (or "sweating") the onions and garlic, creating sweetness and depth. Homemade curry powder keeps well for a few weeks and warms up deviled eggs, beef stew, or hot buttered popcorn.

SERVES 6 TO 8

3 tablespoons unsalted butter
1 medium onion, thinly sliced
2 garlic cloves, sliced
2½ teaspoons kosher salt
2 pounds carrots
1 tablespoon plus 2 teaspoons Curry Powder (recipe follows),
    plus more for garnish
Pinch of cayenne
½ cup dry white wine
Thick Greek-style yogurt, for garnish
½ cup shelled roasted pistachios

Melt the butter in a heavy 4-quart pot. Add the onion, garlic, and ½ teaspoon of the salt. Cover and cook over low heat for 10 to 15 minutes, until the onions are soft and translucent.

Meanwhile, peel the carrots and slice them into thin rounds.

Raise the heat to medium, and add the curry and cayenne. Stir and cook for 1 minute, until fragrant. Add the carrots, wine, and another ½ teaspoon of the salt. Cook for 2 minutes, until the wine reduces a little. Add 6 cups water and the remaining 1½ teaspoons salt. Bring to a simmer, cover, and cook for 25 to 30 minutes, until the carrots are completely tender.

Puree in a food processor or with an immersion blender. Add water if the soup seems too thick. Adjust the seasoning and serve in warm bowls. Garnish with yogurt, the pistachios, and a sprinkling of curry powder.

RECIPE CONTINUES

curry powder

MAKES ABOUT ½ CUP

¼ cup plus 1 tablespoon coriander seeds
1 teaspoon cumin seeds
1 teaspoon black mustard seeds
1 teaspoon fenugreek seeds
1 teaspoon black peppercorns
2 large dried red chiles, such as de árbol
2 tablespoons ground turmeric

In a small pan over medium heat, toast the coriander seeds, cumin seeds, mustard seeds, fenugreek seeds, peppercorns, and chiles, tossing constantly, for about 2 minutes, until fragrant and slightly colored. Let cool completely.

Grind the mixture in a spice mill or clean coffee grinder until very fine. Transfer to a small bowl and stir in the turmeric.

SPRING MOUNTAIN

The first time I met Joe Hollis, he was knocking on our front door at nearly midnight with thirty pounds of ramps in a beat-up cooler. I was looking for wild springtime plants that grow in the mountains a few hours west of here and he was looking for a restaurant customer. He stayed for a cup of tea, and on his way out revealed that his parents had built our house in 1960. Not a sentimental guy, he kindly declined a tour of his old home but was curious how the woods out back were doing. Today we went for a walk there together.

Climbing down onto the trail, beyond the thick mat of invading English ivy from neighborhood gardens, we begin to see the once-a-year native "ephemerals"—plants that appear for just weeks after the earth begins to warm and before the trees above them leaf out and shade them. Joe points out fairy spuds with pale pink blooms that float on skinny stems; bloodroot, white stars that flower for just a day; and a colony of mayapples, their pointed leaves propelling each one up through the dead leaves like an umbrella before opening, and whose white blossoms are followed by a small edible fruit. We see trout lilies (also called dog-toothed violets), which have leaves like a speckled brook trout and orchid-like yellow flowers. Flour made from their tiny tubers is prized in Japan as a silky thickener for subtle broths and stews.

The woods around Joe's house near Black Mountain are slowly coming to life, too. There, Joe is cultivating and foraging for our own distinct *sansai*—the Japanese word for their celebrated native mountain vegetables, many of which have a close relative here in North Carolina. A few rare plants—including a native truffle—grow nowhere else in the world except here and there. Joe forages for fiddlehead ferns; the fresh, creamy hearts of new bamboo; tender shoots of giant solomon's seal; and sweet, crunchy Indian cucumber root. He also cultivates rarities like peppery sansho, the green buds of a tree closely related to the one that produces Sichuan peppercorns; udo, which is similar to white asparagus; and in his stream, pale green wasabi roots and their spicy heart-shaped leaves.

But the very first thing he sends us each spring is ramps, another ephemeral, one that he forages deep in the woods at 3,200 feet, about an hour's hike from his garden. Ramps are a mostly green, broad-leafed wild lily in the same family as onions, but with a delicious garlic edge. Ramps grow best in what Joe calls "coves"—low-lying ground that never dries out and is covered in a thick mulch of hardwood leaves. He cuts them by hand with a sharp pocketknife, leaving their bulbs firmly rooted in the earth so that they come back again year after year.

cast-iron-skillet fresh trout with cornmeal

Not far from Joe's Mountain Gardens in Celo is Canton, a mill town that is home to Sunburst Trout Farm (see Sources, page 264), where Sally Eason raises delicate pink trout in the pure water that rushes down Cold Mountain. If a campfire is not in your immediate future but you have some sparkling fresh trout, this works well on the stovetop, too. Serve it with wilted ramps (page 27) or other greens.

SERVES 4

4 whole trout, about 12 ounces each, cleaned and gills removed
Kosher salt and freshly ground black pepper
2 cups finely ground white cornmeal
Expeller-pressed vegetable oil, as needed

Prepare a hot campfire. Generously season each fish, inside and out, with salt and pepper. Pour the cornmeal onto a large plate and season it generously with salt and pepper.

When the fire dies down, place a grill rack over the bed of embers and assemble everything you will need: your largest cast-iron skillet, the oil, a thick dry towel or sturdy pot holder, a metal spatula, a pair of long tongs to adjust the embers or grill rack if needed, and a serving platter for the fish. When the grill is very hot, the flame has completely died down, and the coals are covered with ash, put the skillet on the center of the grate and let it get hot.

In the meantime, thoroughly coat each fish with a light dusting of cornmeal.

Add ¼ inch of oil to the hot skillet and test the oil: a sprinkling of cornmeal should immediately sizzle. Shake any excess cornmeal from the fish and slowly lay them in the skillet (you may need to work in batches if your skillet is not large enough to fit them all). Keep a close eye on the fish as they cook, and rotate the pan or gently adjust the fish with the spatula and tongs as needed. Cook the fish for 4 to 6 minutes, until crispy and golden brown. Flip them over and continue until cooked through, 2 to 3 minutes. If the pan becomes dry during cooking, add a small amount of additional oil to the skillet.

wilted ramps

On the first day of the year that is warm enough to open the windows, we all instantly crave spring foods. While the asparagus, peas, and strawberries we hunger for lag many weeks behind, the early tonics of spring—spring onions, green garlic, and ramps—step in to give us the jolt we need to wake up from winter.

Wash and dry 2 bunches of ramps, leaving them whole. Heat a few tablespoons of bacon fat or olive oil in a skillet over medium-high heat and then add the ramps. Season well with kosher salt and freshly ground black pepper, and turn them frequently with tongs as they cook until they soften and begin to wilt, a few minutes. Add a splash of red wine vinegar and cook for another few minutes, until the ramps are completely tender.

campfire bacon and eggs in a bag

I ate this magical meal at Girl Scout camp and then thought about it for the next thirty-odd years until we went camping in the mountains near Joe's. It's a full breakfast in a paper bag, easy to make if you already have a campfire burning (or hot embers in a charcoal grill or fireplace), portable, and delicious. As the bacon in the bottom of the paper bag renders and becomes crispy-chewy, the fat protects the paper from burning and gently steams the egg. This cannot be prepared in advance: after the eggs are cracked, the bags should be dangling over the hot coals within a minute. If your mess hall prefers scrambled eggs, they work well, too.

SERVES 6

6 lunch-size paper bags
6 thick slices bacon, cut in half crosswise
6 large eggs
Kosher salt and freshly ground black pepper

Prepare a campfire or a fire in a fireplace or charcoal grill. Let the flames die down and the coals become completely covered with ash. (Don't attempt this on a gas grill—it doesn't have the firepower to render the bacon before the eggs soak the bags.)

Lay 2 bacon halves across the bottom of each bag so that it is completely covered. Reach into each bag and carefully crack an egg over the bacon. Season with salt and pepper. Securely fold down the top of each bag three times and poke a hole through the fold with a sharp skewer. Thread a long, green stick through the hole and hold each bag so that the bottom is as close to the hot embers as possible—but without touching them and nowhere near any open flame. Cook for about 10 minutes, until the egg white is cooked all the way through.

WILD SHRIMP

We surprised the kids with a day at the beach, our mystery destination revealed only when we were on the bridge heading over the Intracoastal Waterway and they spotted boats. Our meal tonight is at a restaurant on the waterway itself, where boaters are docked for dinner, waiting for tables at the outdoor bar with icy beers and boiled shrimp—but the shrimp don't jibe with the scenery. This restaurant, like many here, serves only farm-raised shrimp and frozen flounder when abundant pink shrimp and summer flounder swim just off shore. At coastal seafood restaurants in North Carolina, it can be a challenge to find seafood that is actually from here, and in this we join vacationers up and down the East Coast, eating king crab from Alaska and farmed salmon from Chile. Like German tourists having schnitzel for lunch at the restaurants that line the beaches in Mallorca, we take part in these sunburned evenings in something more ritual than actual meal, a shell of an eating experience.

Not long ago, shrimp was special-occasion food. Now with the availability of vast quantities of inexpensive shrimp made possible by farming, we can eat it nearly as often as we like. Almost all the shrimp we eat in the U.S. is imported from industrial farms in Asia and Latin America, where the industry erodes the local environment and coastal communities. Aquatic monoculture generally requires heavy use of pesticides, antibiotics, and hormones, and because of the high levels of pollution they create, the farms are generally short-lived, moving on after just a few years to new, unspoiled locations.

Industrial farming has transformed shrimp from a seasonal, small-scale, localized specialty into an inexpensive, but far less flavorful, industrial product that also now makes it hard for wild shrimpers to make a living off the original. Farmed shrimp wouldn't be cheap if the producers paid the actual costs of production (you can imagine the credit card ad: "An ancient mangrove forest . . . priceless"). A popular bumper sticker here at the beach reads, "Friends Don't Let Friends Buy Imported Shrimp."

Just-caught wild shrimp from the sea are briny and succulent, one of the most delicious things you can eat, but only a tiny fraction of the shrimp that we eat in the United States is wild. There are wide-ranging regional and seasonal variations: spot prawns on the West Coast in spring and summer; tiny sweet Maine shrimp in the northeast in winter. In North Carolina, we start off with brown shrimp in May and segue into pink or spotted shrimp later in spring and then on to white shrimp (also called green-tails) at the end of August. In great shrimp years, the green-tails hang on all the way through the winter until the brown shrimp are back.

shrimp, pea, and rice stew

The simplest way to enjoy wild shrimp is to cook them fast and serve them warm, still in their shells, with melted butter. This recipe takes the opposite but equally flavorful tack: the shrimp are slow-cooked, infusing the entire soup with sweet shrimpiness.

SERVES 4 TO 6

½ pound wild shrimp (see Sources, page 264), peeled and deveined

2 teaspoons kosher salt

4 large shallots, finely minced (about ½ cup)

¼ cup fish sauce, plus more if needed

1 teaspoon freshly ground black pepper

1 teaspoon sugar

½ cup plus 2 tablespoons jasmine or other aromatic long-grain white rice

2 tablespoons expeller-pressed vegetable oil

3 cups shelled fresh or frozen green peas

1½ cups finely chopped fresh cilantro, leaves and tender stems

1 cup thinly sliced scallions, white and green parts

2 cups chopped tender pea greens or fresh spinach

Salt-clean the shrimp: Put the shrimp in a colander and sprinkle with the salt. Toss with your hands, rubbing gently to make sure all surfaces are evenly covered. Let sit for 5 minutes; then rinse in cold water and drain. Cut each shrimp in half lengthwise and then in half again crosswise. Put the shrimp in a medium bowl and add the shallots, fish sauce, pepper, and sugar. Mix well and let marinate covered at room temperature for 1 hour.

Put the rice into a spice mill and pulse it a few times to grind, about 10 seconds total. The largest grains will be a third of their original size.

Heat the oil over medium-low in a 4-quart pot and add the shrimp mixture. Sauté, stirring frequently, for 3 to 5 minutes, until all the shrimp are pink and the shallots have softened but not colored. Add the rice and stir well. Gradually add 2 quarts water, stirring constantly to avoid clumping. Raise the heat to high and bring the mixture to a simmer. Reduce the heat to medium-low and simmer, stirring often, for 20 to 25 minutes, until the rice is completely tender and the broth has thickened. Raise the heat to high, add the peas, and cook for 3 to 4 minutes, until the peas are just tender; remove from the heat. Add the cilantro, scallions, and pea greens, and season with a splash of fish sauce if necessary.

ASPARAGUS FEAST

Every year in early April, I start hoping for rain and checking my voice mail until I finally get the word from Graham Broadwell that his asparagus are up. It can happen at any moment—in perfect conditions, asparagus spears can grow nearly a foot a day. This afternoon, Graham dropped off our first twenty pounds, enough to send out as a surprise to regulars at the restaurant tonight, and for everyone in the kitchen to take a handful home for a midnight snack. The asparagus arrives arranged upright in white plastic buckets and we unpack it and sort the spears: tiny shoot-like "whips" that are nearly as skinny as their wild cousins, dark purple spears that I put in a big glass vase of icy water on the bar. We fight over the fattest spears, more tender and satisfying than the thinner ones, since most of the fiber is in the skin. If you too like the largest spears best, you know how scarce they can be; hybrid varieties of asparagus are bred to encourage the number of male plants, which while ridiculously more productive and longer living, can be on the skinny side. Many believe that while female plants produce fewer spears (since much of their energy is diverted to producing seed), their low-yield spears are also more robust and succulent. Sorry, guys.

Each Wednesday for the next five or six weeks, Graham and his wife, Sara, will bring us as much asparagus as they are willing to part with. It is an act of kindness and habit; they could sell it all at the Durham farmers' market for a higher price. As the weather warms up, Catbriar Farm's plot of asparagus will be picked every day and our weekly take will soon be sixty pounds. For the next month asparagus will be everywhere at Lantern— pan-roasted with tamari and butter and topped with a poached egg; in a puddle of warm miso with crispy ham and peeled early cherry tomatoes; sliced very thin on the bias and briefly pickled in salt to go with sweet broiled eel. At home we get simple: grilled or boiled and served steaming hot with melted butter and garlic croutons. After nearly six weeks of daily asparagus feasts, I won't really miss eating them for the next ten and a half months.

asparagus with butter and soy

This dish is all about timing: poach the eggs first and keep them in a warm spot.

SERVES 2

Kosher salt
White vinegar
2 large eggs, at room temperature
1 bunch asparagus (about ½ pound), tough ends snapped off
2 teaspoons expeller-pressed vegetable oil
2 tablespoons soy sauce
5 tablespoons unsalted butter, at room temperature
Flaky sea salt, such as Maldon

Fill a medium pot halfway with water and bring it to a boil over high heat. Add enough kosher salt so that the water is as salty as seawater.

Meanwhile, fill a medium saucepan halfway with water, add a small splash of vinegar, and bring to a boil over high heat. Reduce the heat so the water simmers gently. One at a time, crack each egg into a small teacup with a handle and then slowly and gently slide the egg into the simmering water—the rim of the cup should actually dip into the water so that the egg doesn't have very far to fall. Adjust the heat so the water stays at a slow simmer. Cook for 2 to 3 minutes, until the white is just set and the yolk is still runny. Use a slotted spoon to transfer the eggs to a plate.

Heat a 9-inch sauté pan over high heat. When the pan is very hot, drop the asparagus into the boiling water and cook for 25 to 30 seconds, less if the asparagus is very skinny. Drain the asparagus and gently shake them dry. Add the oil to the hot pan and swirl. Immediately add the asparagus and toss constantly for about 30 seconds, until they become slightly blistered in spots. Do not lower the heat. Add the soy sauce and shake the pan to coat the asparagus; as soon as it evaporates, remove the pan from the heat, add 1 tablespoon water, and immediately follow with the butter. Continue to toss the asparagus until the butter is melted, creating a dark golden brown emulsified sauce. If the sauce has broken, add up to a tablespoon of water and continue to toss until it comes back together.

Divide the asparagus and the sauce between two plates, and top each with a warm poached egg. Sprinkle the eggs with a little sea salt.

charcoal-grilled asparagus

As traditionally seasonal delicacies like asparagus, strawberries, and peaches have become everyday food, the idea that they are a treat has somehow stuck—but with none of the flavor or meaning. Year-round asparagus has become a stand-in for a kind of perfunctory idea of good eating—the Whole Foods near us recently installed a permanent granite waterfall shrine to asparagus in their entrance—yet is a shadow of its tasty springtime self.

When you put just-picked asparagus on a hot grill, they are so juicy they actually jump as they start to cook.

Prepare a hot fire in a charcoal grill. Count on 8 to 10 asparagus per person as a side dish or as the focal point of a salad. Keeping all the tips pointing the same direction, toss the asparagus with olive oil, a generous amount of salt, and some freshly ground black pepper. When the flame has died down, the coals are completely covered with ash, and the grill is very hot, grill the asparagus (in batches as necessary). Cook for 2 to 3 minutes per side until fragrant, lightly marked, still vibrant green on the outside, and juicy and tender on the inside.

OUTDOOR BIRDS

Ben Bergmann and Noah Ranells started Fickle Creek Farm to grow vegetables, but they didn't plant their first seeds for market until after nearly four years of farming. For the first two, goats cleared swaths of pasture through their mostly wooded seventy-four acres; for the next two, chickens weeded and fertilized. The pigs came last, tilling the soil, rooting out rocks, and taking care of the weeds the other animals wouldn't touch.

Each animal serves a specific function in the farm's ecosystem and they continue to cycle through their pastures and woodlands, sustainably clearing and feeding the land, allowing Ben and Noah to make do with mainly organic on-farm "inputs"—another way of saying fertilizers (and often pesticides), but in this case meaning composted manure. This spring, they are finally planting fig trees and blueberry bushes and starting beehives. As the years go by, as scrubby undergrowth gives way to new pastures and as the soil becomes richer and healthier, they will eventually need fewer animals. But for now, on cold nights the pole barn—with baby sheep, calves, and goats keeping each other warm—seems an improbable fantasy of farm life that is everyday business here.

Ben and Noah could have cleared their fields in a few weeks with a backhoe and brought fertilizers in from off the farm, but quick and easy isn't really their style. Ten years in, they grow almost everything they eat (making store runs for ice cream and beer) and have fostered fifteen children here on the farm. One of these children, Jerry, was initially brought to the U.S. at age thirteen by a "coyote" from his home in Puebla, Mexico, to work at a Tyson chicken plant. He worked there for three years, until a state inspector dismissed him—not for his age or immigration status, but because he was too short.

At Fickle Creek, farming is a long story of the relationship between land, animals, and plants. Right now, they are in the midst of their egg chapter: a thousand laying hens now live in the woods, where they are putting the finishing touches on some new corridors of pasture for grazing sheep and steers (including some Jersey calves from Chapel Hill Creamery), meandering through shady groves where they will stay cool in the summer heat. These hens lay their eggs in one of five "egg mobiles," portable nesting houses that allow the birds to do their work wherever they are needed. Four waist-high Great Pyrenees dogs stand guard and keep the hens safe from predators day and night, when many choose to roost in the low branches of pine trees under the stars.

Seven different old breeds give a dozen Fickle Creek eggs the farmers-market look, among them there are creamy white eggs from the White Leghorns, pale green Araucana eggs, purple-brown Golden Comets, and dark caramel-brown Red Stars. The variation serves a purpose—some chickens do better in heat, some lay more when it's cold—and helps keep the egg supply consistent.

After about three years on the farm, a laying hen reaches the end of her life. At this age, she might not make it through the stress of the first freeze in the fall or the first 90-degree day of summer. Most critically, she no longer produces enough eggs to pay for the cost of her feed. Every so often, Ben gathers a small group of these birds in a grove of trees behind the barn and gently grasps them by their feet to hang them upside down, putting them into a trancelike state before severing their necks with a just-sharpened knife. This morning there was a gentle breeze and a sense of calm when Ben thanked each hen before concluding their arrangement. They had lived full, chickeny lives—scratched for bugs, taken dust baths, produced nearly a thousand eggs, eaten what they wished—and died just feet from where they arrived at Fickle Creek as day-old chicks. As I helped pluck the feathers, the animals became the chickens that we know in the kitchen, and I started to think about how we would cook them.

hen and dumplings

A laying hen is a different animal from the six- to ten-week-old supermarket fryers, roasters, and broilers we usually see. Laying hens are typically sold between one and three years old and create a different sort of stew, deeper in overall flavor but with less succulent meat. If you are using a laying hen, increase the cooking time to about an hour and a half, or until the meat is very tender. It will not be necessary to remove the breast meat during cooking as directed below.

SERVES 6 TO 8, WITH LEFTOVERS

STEW

1 (4-pound) chicken with neck, gizzard, and heart
3 medium carrots
3 celery stalks
1 small onion, halved
1 head of garlic, unpeeled, cut in half crosswise
2 dried bay leaves
Kosher salt
1 teaspoon black peppercorns
1 large leek, white and green parts cut into a medium
    dice and washed, green top washed and reserved
About 20 sprigs fresh flat-leaf parsley, stems reserved
    and leaves chopped (2 tablespoons) for garnish
¾ cup dry white wine
1 cup heavy cream

DUMPLINGS

2 cups all-purpose flour
1 tablespoon baking powder
1 teaspoon kosher salt
2 large eggs
½ cup buttermilk
8 tablespoons (1 stick) unsalted butter, melted
2 tablespoons chopped fresh flat-leaf parsley
2 tablespoons thinly sliced fresh chives

1 small bunch of fresh chives, cut into ¾-inch batons

Freshly ground black pepper

Put the chicken, neck, gizzard, and heart in a 6-quart heavy pot. Cover with 3 quarts cold water and bring to a simmer over high heat. As the water approaches simmering, begin to skim away any fat or scum. Reduce the heat to medium and simmer for 5 minutes while continuing to skim. Add 1 of the carrots, 1 of the celery stalks, the onion, garlic, bay leaves, 1 tablespoon salt, and the peppercorns. Reduce the heat to low, cover, and simmer for 10 to 15 minutes.

Transfer the chicken to a cutting board. After letting it cool for a few minutes, cut off the breast meat, which ideally should be just done and still slightly pink at the bone. Set the meat aside and return the rest of the chicken to the pot. Simmer gently for 20 minutes over low heat. Add the dark green top of the leek and the parsley stems to the pot, and simmer for 10 minutes.

While the chicken is cooking, dice the remaining 2 carrots and 2 celery stalks.

Remove the legs from the chicken and reserve. Strain the broth—you will have about 2 quarts. Discard the vegetables and bones. Rinse out the pot and pour the broth back into it (off the heat).

Prepare the dumpling batter: Whisk together the flour, baking powder, and salt in a medium bowl. In a small bowl, whisk the eggs, buttermilk, and butter. Add the wet ingredients to the dry. Mix well with a wooden spoon, and then stir in the parsley and chives.

When the chicken legs are cool enough to handle, remove the skin and pick the meat off the bone. Gently tear it into bite-size chunks. Repeat with the reserved breast meat, and set all the chicken meat aside.

Bring the broth to a boil over high heat and add the diced carrots, celery, and leek and the wine. Reduce the heat to medium and cook for 4 minutes, until the vegetables are slightly softened. Add the cream and chicken and bring back to a simmer. Check the seasoning and adjust as necessary.

Using two teaspoons, form dumplings and drop them into the simmering stew, spreading them out. Towards the end of the process, the pot may begin to seem crowded; give it a gentle stir as necessary. When all the dumplings are in the stew, give it another stir, flipping over any dumplings that are not submerged. Cover and simmer for 5 minutes. Remove from the heat, stir in the parsley and the chives, and serve with freshly ground pepper.

raw vegetables
with garlic-anchovy mayonnaise

This was one of the coldest winters here anyone can remember and many producers harvested root vegetables from underneath a cover of snow. It was hard on the farmers but great for the carrots, which didn't get prettier but definitely got sweeter while resting in the cold winter earth. Carrots aside, early spring is the time to eat raw vegetables, especially at Fickle Creek. Gather as many colors, textures, and flavors as you can, such as small fennel, carrots, and radishes but also sweet scallions, baby turnips, and hearts of butter lettuce. Good on their own, they are of course also delicious with homemade mayonnaise. If you have an immersion or stick blender, you can make your own mayonnaise in 2 minutes.

Put the yolks from 2 large, room-temperature eggs in a wide-mouth jar and pulse for about 30 seconds with the blender. Add a good pinch of salt, a little minced garlic, an anchovy fillet or two, and a big squeeze of lemon juice, and pulse again. While pulsing, slowly drizzle in about 1 to 1¼ cups total oil—I like a combination of neutral vegetable oil and a little extra virgin olive oil for flavor—pulsing the blender frequently until the mixture is emulsified. Taste for salt, and thin with a little water if necessary.

MILK MONEY

It's finally spring today; the grass is looking green and my son Arthur's forehead is swollen with mosquito bites. Early this evening, we stopped by Chapel Hill Creamery to watch the evening milking and meet the twin baby oxen that are in training to work together as a team. Less than a year old, they are growing so fast that they are on their third handmade yoke. Herd manager Allison Sturgill helped their mother give birth and is now teaching them to pull a small cart. Earlier today, they pulled a fallen tree out of the woods.

Proprietors Flo Hawley and Portia McKnight wanted to make cheese and so became farmers first. Ten years later, they are a triple threat: cultivators of 37 acres of grass, livestock managers who recognize each of their pasture-raised Jersey cows by her udder, and—when the farm chores are finally done—artisan cheese makers. Their primary concern is the health of their animals, and it shows in the rich, low-yield milk that goes into their cheeses, in the deep flavor of their whey-fed pork and, a few times a year, Jersey beef (the destiny of most of their male calves at about eighteen months). The girls, as the herd is known, have been eating their favorite grasses for a few weeks now—tall rye grass and juicy clover—and their milk is quite changed from winter. The cheeses show it: we take home a soft mozzarella, a brighter yellow than the paler winter variety and still so warm that it barely holds together until dinner.

Portia and Flo are rare examples of farmers getting into, rather than out of, dairy farming. If they had set out to start a dairy farm—perhaps selling bulk milk into a co-op or to a wholesaler—they could not have gone into business at all. Across the country, the prices that dairy farmers are paid for their milk (which, believe it or not, are based in part on a byzantine formula involving commodity cheese prices on the Chicago Mercantile Exchange) are very often actually lower than their costs. These recent lows in dairy prices have resulted in a record loss of dairy farms, but the long-term downward spiral has other causes and consequences. Like the farmers who need to keep increasing production to stay afloat, dairy animals can't keep up themselves. Even though a milking cow may not reach her prime until she is five or six years old, relentless price pressure has created a grim, unsustainable situation in which two-year-olds are slaughtered to make way for each new generation, continually bred for incrementally higher yields. Ever greater quantities of cheaper, less wholesome milk are available, and the milk is produced by fewer, bigger farms that are more reliant on antibiotics and hormones. North Carolina, once a dairy state, is now a milk importer; we continue to lose many dairy farms here each year. Portia and Flo's cheeses are relatively expensive, but when incorporated into a meal, their price comes out in the wash. They would never be able to make it work if their customers weren't willing to pay the real cost of producing their cheese.

Year-round, these cheeses are gentle expressions of their milk. Their Hickory Grove—aged sixty days and buttery with a soft, lacy interior—makes a shockingly good grilled cheese sandwich. Their farmer's cheese is tangy and clean tasting; I like to combine it with buttermilk and herbs in the blender to make a creamy dressing for Bibb lettuce or just toss the cheese as is with salted raw tomatoes and mint. Warm, it becomes soft and oozing in panini (see page 222) or in crisp pastry and transforms a side dish of greens into supper (see page 219).

warm fresh mozzarella with grits, grilled radicchio, and balsamic

If you can't grill the radicchio, just sear it on the stovetop in a cast-iron pan over medium-high heat until it is caramelized and tender.

SERVES 4

1 cup coarse grits (see page 242)
Kosher salt and freshly ground black pepper
Unsalted butter
2 heads of radicchio, trimmed but core left intact, cut in half lengthwise
Extra virgin olive oil
½ teaspoon sugar
¾ pound fresh mozzarella, either in small balls or cut into 4 chunks, at room temperature
Aged balsamic vinegar
Flaky sea salt, such as Maldon

Put the grits in a medium pot, whisk in 5 cups cold water, and season with salt. Bring to a simmer over medium-high heat. Cover and cook, stirring frequently and adding additional water as needed, until they are creamy and tender, 45 minutes to an hour or longer. Add butter to taste and season again with salt.

Meanwhile, prepare a hot fire in a charcoal grill.

Put the radicchio on a large plate and drizzle with olive oil, sprinkle all over with the sugar, and season generously with salt and pepper. When the flame has died down, the coals are completely covered with ash, and the grill is very hot, grill the radicchio, starting with the cut side down, until it is slightly charred on the outside and warm and starting to wilt on the interior, 2 to 3 minutes per side.

Put the mozzarella in a bowl of hot, salted water for 30 seconds to heat and then drain.

Divide the grits among four warm plates, and arrange the cheese and radicchio alongside. Drizzle with balsamic and sprinkle with sea salt.

LOG-GROWN MUSHROOMS

A first-time visitor to Peter Holzman's home garden in the woods north of Chapel Hill might think that she had stumbled upon a working farm, complete with greenhouses, grape arbors, wild persimmon trees, and a 5,000-gallon oil tank repurposed as a cistern. In late spring, the huge yard might contain ten varieties of lettuce, rows of tomatoes, sweet corn just knee-high, heirloom shell beans, and the only artichokes I've seen in the ground outside California. Peter and his partner, Diane, also cultivate shiitake mushrooms, and Arthur and I are visiting today to get a look at the first big "flush," or harvest, of the spring.

While commercial shiitakes are grown in sterilized bags of sawdust, these mushrooms are grown on freshly cut hardwood—and they grow big, dense, and delicious. In recent years, the first week of big spring rains has brought a new crop of mushroom growers— from first-time 4-H Club kids to former tobacco farmers—to Lantern's kitchen door with loads of fantastic, meaty mushrooms for sale. We walk through the woods to Peter's mushroom logs—six hundred in all, mostly oak and sweet gum—stacked into what he calls *ricks:* miniature log cabins with open gaps but no door. I borrow Peter's pocketknife and harvest some shiitakes for our dinner. Peter hosted his annual inoculation party last week, when friends gather in the clearing to help cut fresh green logs, felled for the occasion, into 1-meter lengths, in deference to the Japanese tradition. Once cut, the next step is to drill holes in the wood and use a poker to insert the shiitake plugs deep into the logs. In a few months with the right weather, these new logs will bloom and continue to give about once a season, usually following wet weather, for up to five years.

One reason Peter's mushrooms are so extraordinary is that he doesn't water his logs to trigger a flush; he just waits for nature to take hold. As a result, his shiitakes are low-yield, and so high-flavor. In fact, they are flavorful and rich enough to be eaten raw, shaved with tender celery or fennel and an aged hard cheese and tossed with lemon and parsley. We go back to the house with Diane and simply roast them whole in a hot oven with a little garlic oil and sea salt, set the table with steak knives, and eat the shiitakes with a green salad from the garden, and some rhubarb sorbet I pinched from the restaurant.

roasted shiitake mushrooms with garlic oil

Toss large, fresh shiitake mushroom caps with a generous amount of garlic oil (extra virgin olive oil brought to a simmer with whole smashed cloves of garlic, steeped, then strained), sea salt, and freshly ground black pepper. Put them in one layer on a sturdy sheet pan or in a cast-iron skillet and roast in a 425°F oven for about 10 minutes, or until golden all over, slightly crispy on the edges, but still juicy inside.

pea greens with ume plum vinaigrette and chive blossoms

Pea greens are the immature green tendrils of the pea plant and often have a fresher "pea" flavor than garden peas themselves. Chive blossoms appear here for a few weeks in early spring and add a mellow onion flavor to everything from salad greens, to fresh sashimi, to buttermilk mashed potatoes. To use them, just pull the individual lavender petals off the chive blossom and sprinkle them directly on top of the salad after it is dressed.

For each person, allow about 5 cups loosely packed pea greens and 1 tablespoon Ume Plum Vinaigrette.

ume plum vinaigrette

MAKES ¾ CUP

¼ cup minced shallots
2 tablespoons ume plum vinegar (see Sources, page 264)
3 tablespoons verjus (unfermented juice from wine-quality grapes;
    see Sources, page 264)
1 teaspoon fresh lemon juice
¾ teaspoon sugar
¼ cup plus 2 tablespoons expeller-pressed vegetable oil

Put the shallots in a small bowl and add the vinegar, verjus, lemon juice, and sugar. Let sit for 5 to 10 minutes and drizzle in the oil, whisking. Keeps several days refrigerated.

rhubarb-ginger sorbet

MAKES 1½ CUPS

3 pounds fresh rhubarb, thinly sliced (about 2 quarts)
1½ cups Ginger Syrup (recipe follows)
¼ teaspoon salt
2 tablespoons lemon juice, or more to taste

In a nonreactive saucepan, bring the rhubarb, ginger syrup, and salt to a gentle simmer over medium-low heat. Cook for 10 to 15 minutes, until the rhubarb turns a deep dusky rose color and is the texture of very soft applesauce. Push through a medium (not fine) sieve or colander with a spatula while still warm. It should yield 4 cups. Cool before adding the lemon juice and freezing in an ice cream maker according to the manufacturer's directions.

ginger syrup

This recipe makes a little more ginger syrup than is needed for the sorbet and will keep in the refrigerator for several weeks. It makes an unexpected spring cocktail combined with muddled fresh strawberries, lime juice, and vodka and served over ice.

MAKES 2½ CUPS

2½ cups sugar
2 cups sliced unpeeled fresh ginger

Bring 1¼ cups water to a boil in a nonreactive saucepan. Stir in the sugar and ginger and bring to a very low simmer. Cook for 1 hour. Cool the ginger in the liquid and then strain.

KID-CHURNED ICE CREAM

Instead of taking the kids out for lunch today to celebrate the end of the school year, we made ice cream on the patio. The plan was inspired by the demise of a school garden ice cream social, which is now falling apart for fear of an almighty dessert-at-school backlash. The ice cream that we made today was a nutritious food group all its own: just strawberries, sugar, cream, and buttermilk.

Our work crew—my daughter, Oona; Silvia's daughter, Olivia; Monica's son, Simon; and neighbor Isabel—gathered around a big bowl to crush the whole hulled berries with sugar. The berries now are super-sweet—it hasn't rained and has been warm—and so needed very little extra sweetness. Isabel started off the crush with a sturdy potato masher, but nobody wanted to wait their turn and it was quickly decided that hands would work best anyway. Once the berries were squished (one bowl, eight "impeccably clean" hands), Monica added a little pinch of salt, stirred in equal parts cream and fresh buttermilk, and poured the mixture into the ice cream churn. The kids traded places at the crank with varying levels of effectiveness but the same look of steely determination. Once the cream began to freeze, the crank required more muscular churning from Monica, but from the squishing to the eating, it all took less than forty minutes.

After everyone had a bowl or two of soft, melting ice cream straight from the churn, we sat out on the lawn and ate Mom-mandated bowls of sweet garden peas, which the kids pointed out were actually dessert.

strawberry ice cream

MAKES 2 QUARTS

1 quart ripe fresh strawberries
¾ cup sugar, or more to taste
Pinch of kosher salt
1½ cups buttermilk, preferably full-fat
1½ cups heavy cream

Hull the strawberries, place them in a large bowl, and add the sugar and salt. With a potato masher, coarsely crush the fruit, combining it with the sugar. Stir in the buttermilk and cream, and combine well. Freeze in an ice cream maker.

fresh peas with lettuce and green garlic

SERVES 4

4 tablespoons (½ stick) unsalted butter, at room temperature
5 small stalks green garlic, any tough parts trimmed, sliced into very thin rounds
Kosher salt
1½ cups fresh or frozen shelled green peas
2 small heads of butter lettuce, washed and torn into pieces
Freshly ground black pepper

Melt 2 tablespoons of the butter in a medium sauté pan over low heat. Add the green garlic and a pinch of salt. Cook over low heat, stirring occasionally, for 2 to 3 minutes, until the garlic is tender and fragrant but with no color. Add the peas and cook for 3 to 5 minutes, until they are tender and sweet. Stir in the lettuce and the remaining 2 tablespoons butter; add 1 tablespoon water if the mixture seems dry. Remove the pan from the heat and toss gently until the lettuce wilts and the butter melts. Season with fresh pepper and additional salt if needed.

SEAFOOD MARKET

We are in Barcelona for a few days, eating as much seafood as we can afford. When I ask each waiter we meet where the *gambas* are from, each reliably smiles and gestures vaguely towards the Mediterranean. Together, we silently suspend disbelief: he knows that the big prawns are likely not from the nearby sea, just as I might mention that those waters are essentially barren. I confirm it on the flight home, reading Charles Clover's account of the decline of the oceans, *The End of the Line*. Like most countries, Spain imports much of its seafood from far away; Senegal, for example, licenses foreign trawlers to mine its once bountiful seas, which are increasingly thought to be on the verge of collapse. Like waiting to read Clover's book until after a seafood junket to a once-thriving fishing town, we are all putting off the inevitable future reckoning of the sea.

Is there actually such a thing as sustainable seafood? Much of what was abundant during our grandparents' lifetimes is now overfished and close to collapse, making even the most familiar fish increasingly feel like a nonrenewable resource and those of us who continue to eat fish like the last generation at the table and deep in denial. At the very best, the idea of truly sustainable (as opposed to just relatively less endangered) seafood is a moving target and one that needs to be constantly reassessed.

My own way of dealing with the feeling of helplessness that comes from trying to navigate our evolving picture of the oceans is to focus on what I can feel good about eating instead of what I can't. Tom Robinson helps me do that. His one-room fish market sits in the middle of downtown Carrboro, but it would be at home in the middle of a fishing pier. The cinder-block and concrete room gurgles with constant running water and has a sweet sea smell. Customers bring their papers to the store to recycle and return home with their striper fillets wrapped in last week's news. The fish emulsion from the store goes home with Tom to feed his grove of native persimmon trees, whose fruit is sold in the store alongside fat mullets in the fall. Tom, with his assistant, Salvador, in matching white boots, presides over the only place in town where you could find an African American grandfather, a Japanese housewife, and a grad student from Spain with her small kids in tow, all there to buy fish from someone they trust. Each week, Tom drives to the coast and brings back the best seasonal North Carolina seafood for his devoted customers, who line up before the shop opens each morning to buy fresh head-on shrimp, oysters, soft-shell crabs, speckled sea trout, pound-net flounder, shad roe, live blue crabs, and fresh squid—and to chew the fat. Without Tom, none of us would know how to kill an eel, which coastal congressman to blame for selling violations of the Clean Water Act and the fish kills that result, or exactly what mullets eat in the fall to make them so fatty and sweet.

At Lantern, we try to serve mainly fish and shellfish from relatively nearby and focus on eating as low on the food chain as we can: fast-growing, short-lived species like Spanish mackerel, Atlantic squid, butterfish, wild shrimp, blue crab, sea trout, porgy, black drum, and dried, salted, or tinned anchovies. We also buy from aqua-culture that is thoughtful, local, and well managed, including clams, oysters, mussels, and catfish. In addition to weekly deliveries from Tom, we source from small companies who have their own boats and traps that bring in black drum, porgy, wild shrimp and blue crab and bountiful species from far-off fisheries that are well-managed, resulting in Alaskan sable or "black cod," in Alaska, farmed Arctic char, and wild striped bass from all up and down the east coast. A good beginning rule of thumb is to avoid seafood on Monterey Bay Aquarium's Seafood Watch "red list" (see Sources, page 264).

Tom laughs when I walk through his door brandishing words like "sustainable" and "depleted." He says that the situation at the coast is too complicated to describe in a word. Earlier this afternoon, when I went to pick up Lantern's order and get something for dinner at home, I asked if he considers black bass overfished. His response included a discussion on the hypocrisy of bureaucrats who kill more fish by rubberstamping untenable coastal development or by failing to protect critical estuaries and spawning grounds than fishing quotas can hope to save and a casual reference to fishing restrictions as cultural genocide. Loud talk of agricultural runoff and fish kills would not help most businesses, but Tom is passionate about the dangerous state of seafood, happy to embrace the complexities and contradictions, and honest about his bias. A conversation with him shows that another good way to get fish that you want to eat is to befriend an expert who is fun to talk to and argue with and is willing to reveal his own stake in the game.

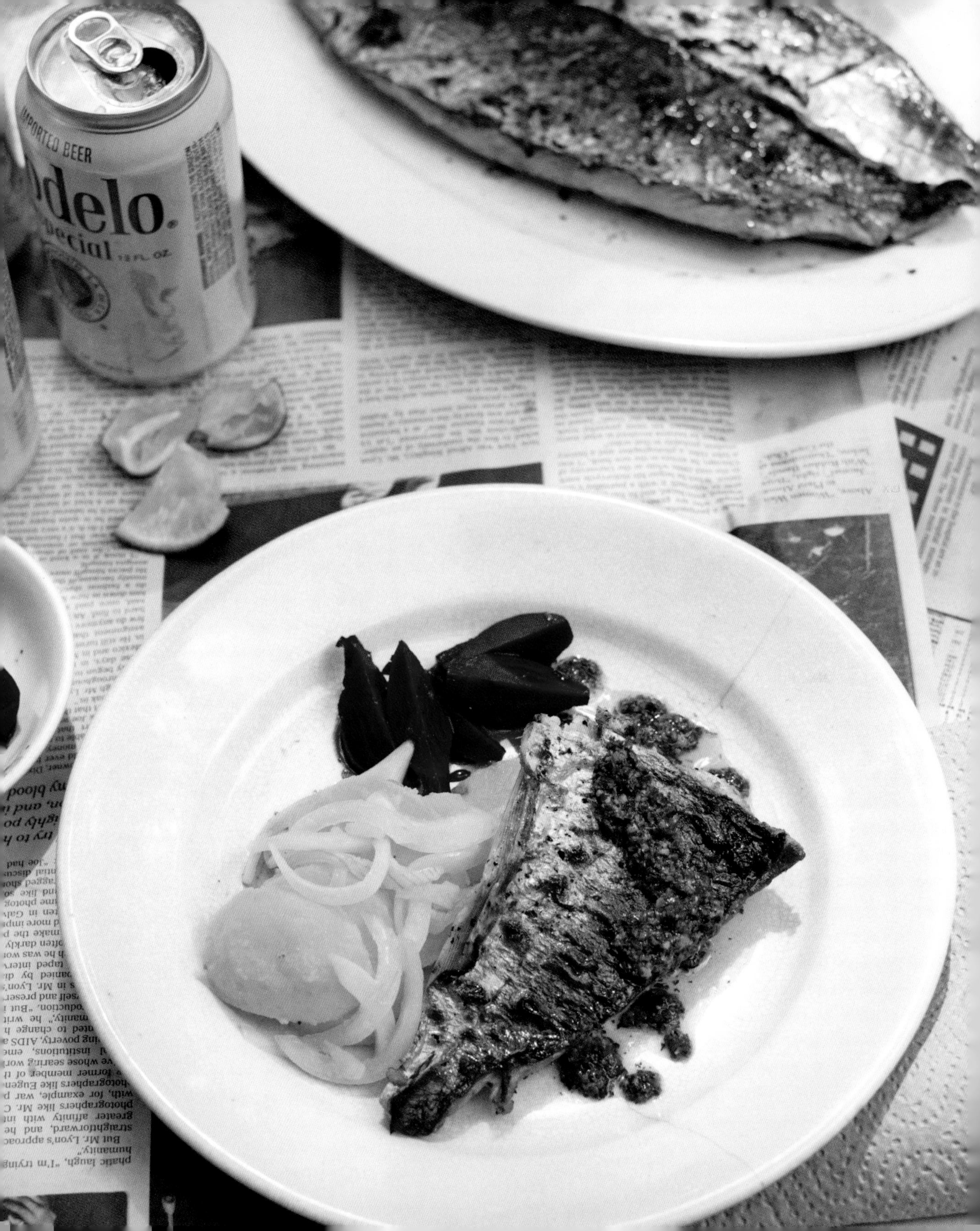
IMPORTED BEER

grilled spanish mackerel with green sauce

The fact that our great-grandchildren may never eat a real seafood dinner gives those of us who still eat fish a responsibility not to put blue cheese on it. I like to serve this with pickled beets (page 142) and the potato salad that follows. This treatment would work for almost any flavorful, rich fish.

SERVES 4

4 (8-ounce) Spanish mackerel fillets, skin on
Kosher salt and freshly ground black pepper
Finely ground dried red chiles, such as de Arbol
Extra virgin olive oil
Green Sauce (recipe follows)

Prepare a fire in a charcoal grill.

Season both sides of each fillet generously with salt, pepper, and chile. Drizzle both sides with a little olive oil.

When the grill is very hot but the flame has died down and the coals are completely covered with ash, put the mackerel, skin side down, on the grill. Cook for at least 2 minutes before moving it at all. In the meantime, watch for flare-ups, extinguishing them with a little water from a squirt bottle (beer works, too). It will take 4 to 6 minutes to cook the skin side. When the skin is crispy and deep golden brown, gently flip the fillets with a spatula and again don't move. Grill for 2 to 3 minutes, until just cooked through. Serve with green sauce.

RECIPE CONTINUES

green sauce

MAKES 1 GENEROUS CUP

2 cups loosely packed fresh flat-leaf parsley leaves

1 cup loosely packed mixed fresh tender herb leaves, such as dill, tarragon,
    chives, lemon balm, basil, spearmint, chervil, and/or fennel fronds

2 scallions, white and green parts, thinly sliced

1 tablespoon finely chopped brined capers

2 oil-packed anchovy fillets, finely chopped

1 hard-boiled egg yolk, finely grated

¼ teaspoon kosher salt

Freshly ground black pepper

Chile flakes

½ cup extra virgin olive oil, plus more as needed

Grated zest and juice of ½ lemon

Chop the parsley, herbs, and sliced scallions very fine. Put them in a small bowl and add
the capers, anchovies, egg yolk, salt, pepper, and chile flakes to taste. Mix well, and slowly
drizzle in the oil, stirring. Add the lemon zest and juice. If the sauce seems too thick, add a
touch more oil. Adjust the seasoning if needed.

potato salad

SERVES 4 TO 6 AS A SIDE DISH

⅓ cup champagne vinegar
Kosher salt and freshly ground black pepper
1 teaspoon sugar
¼ cup olive oil
1½ tablespoons walnut oil
1 medium onion, thinly sliced
1½ pounds (about 8) medium Yukon Gold potatoes

Whisk together the vinegar, 1 teaspoon salt, black pepper to taste, the sugar, and both oils in a small bowl. Add the onion and toss to coat.

Put the potatoes in a medium pot and cover with cold water; add a big pinch of salt. Bring to a boil over high heat and then reduce the heat to a simmer. Cook for about 12 minutes, until the potatoes are easily pierced with the tip of a sharp knife but are still firm. Drain the potatoes, and as soon as they are cool enough to handle, rub the skins off by using a clean tea towel or peel them with a sharp paring knife. Slice the potatoes into ⅓-inch-thick slices and put in a large bowl. Pour the onion mixture over the warm potatoes and combine gently with your hands. Taste for seasoning, and add more salt if necessary.

crispy pan-fried catfish with hot slaw

Frying fish in peanut oil (like using lard for fried chicken) gives catfish the crispiest, least greasy coating imaginable.

SERVES 4

4 catfish fillets (1½ pounds total)
1 cup buttermilk
Kosher salt and freshly ground black pepper
1 cup all-purpose flour
1 cup fine white cornmeal
Pinch of cayenne, or to taste
Peanut oil, for frying
Lemon wedges
Hot Slaw (recipe follows)

Cut the catfish fillets in half lengthwise, and then cut each half diagonally into 2 or 3 long pieces. Pour the buttermilk into a wide, shallow bowl and season it with ½ teaspoon salt and some black pepper. Marinate the catfish in the buttermilk at room temperature for 1 hour.

In another wide, shallow bowl, combine the flour, cornmeal, 1 teaspoon salt, the cayenne, and black pepper to taste.

Drain the catfish in a colander, and lay the pieces on a plate. Season them with ½ teaspoon salt. Pour about 1 inch of peanut oil into a deep cast-iron skillet and heat it to 350°F over medium heat. In batches, roll the catfish pieces in the flour mixture and gently lay them in the hot oil, being careful not to crowd the pan. Cook for about 4 minutes, until golden brown, and then gently flip; cook for 3 minutes or so. When the pieces are evenly crisp and golden brown, transfer them to a clean brown paper bag to drain. Repeat until all the catfish has been fried. Serve with lemon wedges and hot slaw.

hot slaw

SERVES 4 WITH LEFTOVERS

1 medium head of red cabbage, cored and thinly sliced (about 16 cups)

Juice of 1 lemon

Juice of 1 lime

1½ teaspoons raw cane sugar (white may be substituted)

2 teaspoons kosher salt, or more to taste

2 small serrano chile peppers, finely chopped (seeds removed if less heat is desired)

1 large red onion, cut in half and sliced lengthwise into ¼-inch-wide slices

1 garlic clove, smashed and peeled

1 tablespoon expeller-pressed vegetable oil

4 tablespoons (½ stick) unsalted butter

2 bunches fresh cilantro, coarsely chopped (⅔ cup)

In a medium bowl, combine the cabbage with the lemon and lime juices, sugar, salt, and serrano chile. Let marinate for at least 15 and up to 30 minutes.

In a large sauté pan over medium-high heat, sauté the onion and garlic in the oil for 2 to 3 minutes, until fragrant and just starting to color. Raise the heat to high, add the cabbage mixture, and toss until very hot but still crisp, 2 to 3 minutes. Remove the pan from the heat and add the butter and cilantro, tossing well to combine. Taste and season with salt if necessary. Serve hot.

pan-roasted clams with sake

SERVES 2

2½ pounds small littleneck or Manila clams
1 tablespoon expeller-pressed vegetable oil
½ cup sake
4 tablespoons (½ stick) unsalted butter, at room temperature
1 cup thinly sliced scallions, white and light green parts
Kosher salt, if needed

Scrub the clams thoroughly with a brush under cold running water. Drain them in a colander and pat them dry with a paper towel.

Heat a large sauté pan over high heat. When the pan is very hot, add the oil and immediately add the clams. Give them a shake, and cook for one minute. Add the sake, and cover with a tight-fitting lid. Cook for another minute, shaking the pan every 10 seconds. Check the clams: If most of them are open, cover again until all the clams are open, again shaking the pan a little. If only a few have opened, lower the heat and continue to cook, removing clams as they open.

When all the clams have opened, remove the pan from the heat and add the butter (and any clams you removed). Add the scallions and swirl until all the butter is melted. Taste, and season with salt if necessary.

crab and garlic fried rice

SERVES 4 AS AN APPETIZER

4 cups cooked long-grain white rice, refrigerated for at least 1 to 2 days

2 tablespoons clarified butter

2 tablespoons chopped garlic

1 teaspoon kosher salt

5 large egg yolks, beaten well

6 ounces lump crabmeat, picked over for cartilage and shells (about 1 cup)

Take the rice out of the refrigerator 30 minutes before cooking.

Heat a small cast-iron skillet over medium heat. Add the butter and as soon as that gets hot, add the garlic. Cook for 1½ minutes, stirring often, until the garlic is fragrant and just starting to turn light golden. Do not let it brown. Add the rice and salt, stir, and reduce the heat to low. Cover and cook for 3 minutes, stirring every 30 seconds or so, until the rice is hot. Remove the lid and add the egg yolks. Stir continuously for about 2 minutes. Don't let the egg form a crust on the bottom of the pan—the idea is to coat all the rice with the egg and to let the egg just set but not scramble. The rice should look moist. Add the crabmeat and cook for 30 seconds. Remove from the heat, cover, and let rest for 1 minute before serving.

summer

SALT-MARINATING PAGE 68
  Tomato Tasting
  Spicy Melon Salad with Peanuts and Mint

LEMON VERBENA PAGE 74

GOOD DIRT PAGE 75
  Cream of Tomato Soup with Tomato Leaves

COMMUNITY SUPPORTED PIE AND BREAD PAGE 78
  Monica's Blackberry and Summer Apple Pie

BIRTHDAY FEAST PAGE 83
  Spicy Crab and Shrimp Boil with Corn and Potatoes

CHERRIES PAGE 85
  Squab with Grilled Red Onion and Sweet Cherries
  The Homeward Angel
  Pickled Sour Cherries
  Cherry Stone Panna Cotta

CORN PAGE 91
  Crispy Corn Fritters
  Mexican Corn on the Cob

SCHLEPPING FOOD PAGE 94
  Broiled Baby Zucchini with Parmesan
  Grilled Zucchini with Mint, Chile Oil,
    and Toasted Pine Nuts
  Zucchini "Noodles" with Ricotta
  Slow-Cooked Squash with Butter and Basil

OLD BREEDS PAGE 100
  Fried Chicken
  Green Beans with Garlic Bread Crumbs and Tomatoes
  Chilled Berry Pudding with Cream

EGGPLANT AND OKRA PAGE 106
   Eggplant Salad with Walnuts and Garlic
   Fried Okra with Indian Spices and Hot Tomato Relish

TOMATO MAINTENANCE PAGE 111
   Tomato Sandwich
   Kathe's Baked Plum Tomatoes with Olive Oil
      and Bread Crumbs
   Tomato Juice
   Michelada

PEPPERS PAGE 117
   Marinated Roasted Peppers in a Jar
   Flash-Fried Shishito Peppers with Sea Salt

KILLING CRABS PAGE 120
   Garlic and Black Pepper Soft-Shell Crabs
   Cucumber Salad with Lemon Basil
   Watermelon Jell-O with Gin

SHELLING PARTY PAGE 128
   Warm Edamame with Seven-Spice Powder

BACKYARD FRUIT PAGE 132
   Edith Calhoun's Pickled Figs
   Broiled Ripe Figs with Warm Ricotta and Honey

ICEBOX PICKLES AND MORE PAGE 137
   Pickled Carrots and Fennel with Dill and Coriander
   Pickled Pumpkin
   Salt-Cured Chiles
   Chile Oil
   Pickled Chile Peppers
   Pickled Beets
   Pickled Green Tomatoes
   Sauerkraut

SALT-MARINATING

Waking up this morning in the house of a card-carrying foodie, I am asked what I want to cook for breakfast. "Fried eggs?" is not the right answer. My host has ideas: we could sous vide the eggs, roll them in bread crumbs, and deep-fry them in oil or maybe some duck fat, and eat them with a new artisanal harissa. Jonathan is excited to have a fellow foodie in his kitchen, someone he has correctly predicted will be into his extensive honey collection. He cooks for at least a couple hours every day, and his style requires that he consider what seems like every conceivable ingredient option in each meal, regardless of season. His pantry runneth over with crazy ingredients, oils, and essences. He thinks mainly of food but never seems satisfied, preferring to analyze ways in which each meal could have been better or more creative.

My neighbor Sam is Jonathan's opposite. She avoids cooking whenever possible; packaged convenience foods dominate in her kitchen. Raw ingredients, even ones as basic as a fresh carrot or a piece of cheese that isn't pregrated, are in short supply. Despite the extreme simplicity of the meals I usually make at my house, she is intimidated when she comes over to eat. She has come to believe that cooking dinner for her family or friends requires special skills and training.

Food has been mystified and complicated by foodie-ism—the acquisitive, competitive ratcheting up of cooking as entertainment, lifestyle, and identity. It has made us feel we should work much harder to feed ourselves well than we really have to.

When I sprinkle sea salt on freshly dug onions, I think of both Sam and Jonathan. Sam, having them on rye crackers with smoked bluefish and fresh cream cheese, marvels that the salting was all the "cooking" that was done. Jonathan, eating the onions as a condiment with a grilled pork chop, is unimpressed: "You didn't *do* anything!" Stuck between these two extremes, I think an entire meal of salt-marinated dishes would work as dinner for Jonathan and Sam if (no!) they were ever at my house on the same night.

Ripe, thin-skinned summer vegetables love to be quickly marinated in salt before serving. They can be eaten as is or used in other dishes. Some ideas from this week at the farmers' market: a salad of thinly sliced baby squash and chives dressed with oil; green beans, sliced diagonally and combined with toasted sesame seeds as a crunchy side for a softly set Japanese-style omelet; super-sweet cherry tomatoes and basil, crushed in a glass, with good gin and a splash of soda as an addictive savory cocktail.

Cucumbers, onions, and tomatoes are among the most versatile members of the salt-loving team. My favorite cucumber is the ridged Suyo Long, which is super-tender and nearly seedless, but any fresh, thin-skinned unwaxed cuke is good in my book: small gherkins or Kirbys in the beginning of the season, golf ball–size lemon cucumbers, or pale green Armenians, which add a contrasting sweetness to mixed cucumber salads. Fresh "eating" onions like sweet Vidalias work very well, but so do white or purple and green bulbing spring onions, slim fresh scallions, and the papery bronze-skinned yellow "keepers" of winter. With tomatoes, the riper the better, and that almost always means ones from a farmers' market or roadside stand that have never been refrigerated.

Salted cucumbers or onions

Put thinly sliced, diced, or minced cucumbers or onions in a bowl, season generously with kosher salt, and let sit at room temperature until wilted, about 20 minutes and up to an hour. Drain the accumulated liquid before using.

Using salted cucumbers

Serve hefty spears of lightly salted cucumbers upright in a glass alongside cocktails, or as thick slices in a sandwich with fresh cream cheese. Cut them into large dice, sauté briefly in butter, and combine with a tender herb like tarragon or mint as a side for barely cooked wild salmon. Chop them for a fresh green salsa with green chiles, garlic, and a little lime juice. Add salted cucumbers to salted onions (or scallions), a fresh herb like cilantro or dill, drained yogurt, and a warm toasted spice such as cumin or mustard seeds for a sauce or salad.

Combine salt-marinated yellow onion rings with thinly sliced oranges to make a sweet stuffing for a savory baked whole fish. Finely diced salted red onion will garnish a creamy soup or become a speedy chutney when combined with lemon juice and a little cayenne pepper. Rings of salted fresh mild onions add sweet crunch to a green salad with spicy Russian dressing. Thinly sliced salted scallion rounds elevate broiled cheddar cheese on rye.

SALTED TOMATOES

Allowing cut tomatoes to sit with some salt before serving makes them juicier and makes the distinct flavor of each variety even more pronounced. During the summer, we eat some kind of salted raw tomatoes nearly every day—in wedges with creamy hunks of farmer's cheese; sliced and topped with wilted red onions; thinly sliced with hot green chiles and salted cucumbers; or cubed in a big bowl with chunky bacon, a bit of torn romaine, croutons, and a peppery buttermilk dressing. If you cut perfectly ripe tomatoes into small chunks before salting, they become a fast sauce or condiment for hot noodles with a little pounded garlic and oil or, with mint and feta, for skinny grilled Japanese eggplant.

tomato tasting

My favorite way to use them is in a "tomato tasting" salad: Assemble as many varieties, colors, shapes, and sizes of very ripe tomatoes as you can find. Choose a few different "cuts" for variety; for example, cut small yellow pears in half lengthwise to reveal their curves, big beefsteaks in large rectangular chunks, small ridged ones crosswise in thick slices, and some of different colors in small wedges. Arrange them in groups on a long shallow platter and season generously with salt, fresh pepper, and olive oil. As your guests hover expectantly, let the tomatoes sit for at least 30 minutes and up to an hour. Serve with a spoon for the juices.

My dad, Vince, prefers his tomatoes in big rounds, seasoned generously with sea or kosher salt and freshly ground black pepper, and layered on top with thinly sliced red onion, a good quantity of olive oil, and a little red wine vinegar, with bruised fresh oregano leaves strewn over the top. With the tomatoes, Vince serves a grilled flank steak that he has marinated in spicy mustard since morning.

spicy melon salad
with peanuts and mint

In this recipe, fish sauce stands in for the salt to make a savory-sweet spicy salad or side dish. If possible, include two or more types of melon for variety. We get most of our melons from Whitted Bowers, a biodynamic orchard and farm just north in Cedar Grove that also offers a spin on U-pick berries: dig-your-own Carolina Ruby sweet potatoes. Cheri Whitted and Rob Bowers grow many melons; my favorites include the musky Emerald Gem (considered the finest melon in the world after it was developed in 1886), Pride of Wisconsin, and Sugar Baby, the icebox-size watermelon.

SERVES 4

¼ cup fresh lime juice (from about 2 limes)
1 large fresh red Thai chile, with seeds, finely minced, or to taste
¼ cup fish sauce
1 tablespoon sugar, plus more if needed
2 small ripe melons
10 fresh spearmint leaves, torn into thin strips
3 tablespoons chopped salted roasted peanuts

In a medium bowl, combine the lime juice, chile, fish sauce, and sugar with 2 tablespoons water. Stir to dissolve the sugar. Cut each melon in half and remove the seeds. Using a melon baller, scoop out the flesh to make about 4 cups melon balls total. Add the melon balls to the dressing and toss. Let marinate in the refrigerator for at least 45 minutes and up to several hours.

To serve, toss with the mint, divide among four bowls, and sprinkle with the peanuts.

LEMON VERBENA

Whenever we get a bucket of lemon verbena from Bill Dow, former doctor and for thirty years now a farmer on his Ayrshire Farm, its powerful scent takes over the kitchen and has me woozy trying to come up with different ways of using it. It's one of those delicious aromatic herbs like winter savory, lavender, and rau ram (Vietnamese cilantro)—intoxicating when held in a big fresh bunch but tough to take as the main flavor in a meal. Lemon verbena goes well with summer fruits like watermelon and peaches, adds a mystery flavor when stuffed inside a roast chicken, and makes a fine sherbet. It's easy to grow, and if you find yourself with a bumper crop on the eve of the first frost, it is simple to preserve it by grinding the leaves along with some white sugar in a food processor until it combines into aromatic, bright green sand. The sugar will last perfectly for months in the freezer and can be used to flavor drinks, ice creams, custards, and fruit compotes.

When we have lots, like today, I make an infusion and drink it all afternoon: Put a handful of fresh leaves into a pot or heatproof pitcher, cover with boiling water, and allow it to steep briefly; no need to strain. It's good hot or chilled as a refreshing tonic. You can sweeten it with a little honey or raw sugar, but it's not necessary.

GOOD DIRT

The act of composting is both generous and thrifty, fueling two fundamental urges of any good cook. Composting makes a better, messier, and bolder cook, undeterred by carrots with long tops, bunches of greens with big stems, or a cabbage with a bruise. Thinking about a freshly dug onion as a whole—the part that you eat and the other part that you deposit back into the ground to grow new dirt—fosters a connection to where it came from and also, somehow, more patience for slicing it. The skin and roots that were once trash have a new kind of value when composting them closes the circle. Once in a garbage bag, an apple core or coffee grounds are sentenced to the landfill forever; composting liberates food by keeping its nutrition with us, generating future fertility. At the restaurant, we pay more attention to how we use ingredients as we watch the big bin of stems, leaves, eggshells, and citrus skins grow during the prep day. Avoiding the garbage and feeding the compost bin (or a bucket earmarked for EcoFarm's pigs) makes cooking more satisfying.

Before you do it yourself, composting can seem farfetched. In the 1980s, I had a friend who devoted an entire bathroom in her Chelsea loft to what was more art installation than vermiculture. After dinner, guests would sit giggling or cringing on the edge of her tub to feed their food scraps to her worms. With no garden to mulch, she would use her worm castings to discreetly mulch the gingko trees on her block. I didn't get her compulsion until ten years later, when I realized how simple it could be with even a small amount of outdoor space.

A simple open bin or two-foot-square pile can hold a year's worth of scraps. Our pile is just a stack behind a tree, where we toss scraps and cover them with a handful of dead leaves. We collect the scraps in an old enamel stock pot with a heavy lid set next to the garbage can on the floor. It is becoming more common for cities to offer curbside compost pickup along with the trash. Other urban composters keep a big zip-top bag in the freezer to collect trimmings that they drop off at a nearby community garden or farmers' market. If you don't happen to have a spare tub, it is simple to create a small worm bin that fits underneath a kitchen sink. In the summertime, fruit flies are easily handled using a simple homemade trap baited with an overripe banana (see photo, page 76), although the device seems a little less magical since I found out that the bananas are a likely source of my flies to begin with.

My hands-off approach—I don't take the compost's temperature, worry about the precise proportion of green to brown, or even turn it over with a pitchfork—makes for a long-term project. Last week we used a vintage layer from 2005. As we dug it out, Oona and Arthur played archeologists hoping to uncover an ancient tomb, but our most exciting discoveries were a wine cork and a couple of clamshells. We used the soil, as moist and crumbly as warm chocolate cake, to feed some potted plants on the patio and watered it in. Today there is a deep green mat of robust tomato volunteers growing in each pot—the soil must have been dug from a late-summer stratum of the compost pile, when we were eating tomatoes every day. The pungent green aroma from the seedlings reminds me that my first memory of tomatoes isn't of eating them but of my mom bending over our backyard tomato plants, showing me how to snap off the suckers—the stems that will never flower. Tomatoes seem like the garden plant most affected by the quality and complexity of the earth in which they are grown: the spicy, herbal smell of their stems and leaves, bound with the sweet-smelling dirt, is more tomato-y than a tomato itself.

cream of tomato soup
with tomato leaves

We had too many seedlings to plant and so Monica also used them for the dessert for a tomato dinner: sweet tomato gelée and cream garnished with the tiny leaves. The tomato soup here also gets an assist from larger stems and leaves that are removed at the end, but very small, tender leaves from young plants (or volunteer seedlings) make a nice garnish as well.

SERVES 8 TO 10

4 pounds (about 20) very ripe plum tomatoes, peeled, halved, and seeded, juice reserved
Kosher salt
3 tablespoons unsalted butter
2 cups minced onions (about 3 small)
2 large garlic cloves, minced
1 tablespoon all-purpose flour
¼ cup dry sherry
1 tablespoon tomato paste
⅛ teaspoon cayenne pepper
½ cup heavy cream
2 cups whole milk
A handful of tomato stems with leaves
Freshly ground black pepper

Cut the tomatoes into ¼-inch cubes, put them in a bowl, and season with 1 teaspoon salt.

Melt the butter in a heavy nonreactive pot over low heat. Add the onions and garlic and season with 1 teaspoon salt. Sauté the vegetables for 12 to 15 minutes, until they are soft.

Raise the heat to high, stir in the flour, and cook for 1 to 2 minutes. Pour in the sherry and scrape the bottom of the pan as it bubbles away. Stir in the tomato paste. Add the tomatoes and their juice, 2 teaspoons salt, and the cayenne. Reduce the heat to medium-low and simmer for 10 minutes, until the tomatoes are tender.

Stir in the cream and then the milk. Reduce the heat to low and cook for 5 minutes. Remove from the heat and add the tomato stems. Let steep for 10 minutes; then remove and discard the stems.

Before serving, reheat and check the soup for seasoning. Add a little water if the soup seems too thick, and serve with freshly ground pepper at the table.

COMMUNITY SUPPORTED PIE AND BREAD

We are having pie for dinner tonight, a tribute to my friend Phoebe Lawless's annual Pie Fantasy, a depraved Sunday afternoon devoted to pie: salt-roasted beet, chorizo—sweet potato, alongside honeysuckle-chess.

Possessing no natural baking instincts, I am lucky to know not one but two relentless and generous bakers: Phoebe and Lantern pastry chef Monica Segovia-Welsh. Both work on a CSA (Community Supported Agriculture) model, whereby customers sign up and subscribe to a prepaid share of the producer's weekly harvest. Monica and her husband, Rob, practice CSB (Community Supported Bread) and Phoebe provides subscriptions for CSP (Community Supported Pie).

CSB AT JOHNNYS

Chicken Bridge Bakery has a stand at a weekly bootleg farmers' market that convenes at Johnnys, a former bait and sporting goods shop that sold chain saws and night crawlers until new management changed the focus to produce, farm eggs, and tasty coffee. It's become a landing spot for taco trucks and weekly al fresco dinner happenings like whole-hog barbecue and grilled pizza. A corkboard behind the register displays index cards with house accounts where kids can charge their chocolate milk and Popsicles. Each week, Rob and Monica supply sixty families with their daily bread and more: homemade bagels, a delicious loaf from the malty roasted "spent" grain left from a local brewery's beer making, and a rye that uses Foggy Ridge cider to create a sweet, dark crust. It's all baked in a "cob" oven—a homemade clay oven—they built at their house, close to where they raise a flock of chickens and ducks, who provide eggs for corn bread and sourdough English muffin sandwiches. The stand next door is Small Potatoes Farm, where Simon Rose and Natasha McCurley have been farming for just a few years. Aside from fantastic potatoes, they raise chickens, goats, and cows and make their own cheeses for their CSA members. With Monica and Rob, they have created their own food ecosystem, providing heirloom tomatoes and garlic roasted in the Chicken Bridge oven for fougasse, and creating naan using raw goat-milk kefir.

CSP at Durham Farmers' Market

A subscription to Phoebe's Scratch Baking CSP will get you enough pie, sweet or savory, for the week and may include chicken potpie, braised celery pie with anchovy bread crumbs, and a kale pie with homemade guanciale. Her pie obsession runs deep, but at her stand at the Durham market she also sells her homemade pigs in the blanket, muskmelon limeade, and a green tomato stromboli that her fellow Jersey girls can only wish we had grown up with at our neighborhood pizza places. Like Monica and Rob, Phoebe gets most of her ingredients from fellow vendors: pasture-raised pork, freshly milled soft wheat flour, and field peas from the Brinkleys; eggs from Doug Brown, part-time farmer and full-time Durham cop; freshly rendered deep yellow chicken fat from Coon Rock Farm; and a menu of seasonal backyard fruit and nuts like rhubarb, figs, pecans, gooseberries, native persimmons, and chestnuts, which farmers often just let her pick for the price of a pie or two.

Back to pie night at my house . . . Because rolling out the dough for blackberry pie is as much pastry as I can handle in one day, I am ad-libbing a fast crust that uses a few slices of bread to give it solid footing. I first made a rich custard "pie" like this in early spring with members of the lily family—spring onions, green garlic, and leeks—but it works any time of the year with many ingredients, like a mix of mushrooms or very thinly sliced cauliflower with ham and creamy cheese.

monica's blackberry and summer apple pie

Monica makes the best, most intense fruit pies I have ever eaten, so good that her friends beg for birthday pie instead of cake. She keeps the kids happy while the pie cools with "whim wham": While the pie is baking, take the rolled-out dough scraps, sprinkle them with cinnamon-sugar or fold a little jam inside, and bake until browned.

MAKES 1 (9-INCH) DOUBLE-CRUST PIE

CORNMEAL CRUST

2 cups all-purpose flour

⅔ cup stone-ground cornmeal

3 tablespoons confectioners' sugar

1 teaspoon kosher salt

1¼ cups (2½ sticks) unsalted butter, cut into pieces, cold

5 to 7 tablespoons ice water

FILLING

4 cups fresh blackberries

1 large or 2 small tart summer apples or Granny Smith, unpeeled, cored, and sliced into ¼-inch slices (2 cups)

1 cup granulated sugar, depending on the tartness of the fruit

3 tablespoons powdered tapioca or cornstarch

1 teaspoon fresh lemon juice

Pinch of kosher salt

Combine the flour, cornmeal, confectioners' sugar, and salt in a bowl and mix with a spatula. Using a pastry cutter or two knives, cut in the butter. (Alternatively, you can use a food processor.) The butter chunks should vary from pea-size to quarter-size. Drizzle in 5 tablespoons ice water and stir with the spatula. Add another tablespoon or so of ice water if the mixture seems too dry. The dough should not be coming together too much at this point. Next, dump the mixture onto a clean work surface, and using the floured heel of your hand, smear the dough to incorporate. Gather up the dough and do this once or twice more, just until it comes together and you can see streaks of butter throughout. Divide the dough in half and form into 2 loose balls. Wrap them in plastic wrap and press down to flatten the dough into two ½-inch thick disks. Refrigerate for a couple of hours or overnight, until well chilled.

Preheat the oven to 400°F.

Remove dough from the refrigerator and allow to sit at room temperature for 10 to 15 minutes. Combine all the filling ingredients in a bowl and let sit while you roll out your pie crust.

Using a rolling pin on a lightly floured surface, roll each disk to ⅛-inch thickness. Line a 9-inch pie tin with one round of dough, add the filling, and cover with the other round of dough. Crimp the edges with a fork or pinch them with your fingers to seal, removing any excess dough. Cut about five vents around the top of the pie to allow the steam to escape.

Bake the pie in the lower third of the oven for 30 minutes. Then reduce the oven temperature to 350°F, slip a baking sheet underneath the pie tin to catch any bubbling juices, and bake for another 30 to 45 minutes. The pie crust should be nice and browned and the juices should be bubbling through the vents. Pull the pie out and let it cool before cutting.

BIRTHDAY FEAST

If you are lucky enough to know someone with a house and a dock on a bay, there is no more rewarding dinner than this: Bait a wire crab pot and throw it off the dock. Swim, read, fall asleep. Return to the house and drink a beer. Bring water to a boil in the largest pot you can find and get friends to pull up the trap, now full of crabs, and shuck some corn. Add small potatoes to the pot, then the crabs and corn, cover, and let it all steam for a little while. Dinner is served.

During childhood summers at the Jersey shore, my grandmother Marie would casually crab with a single line tied to a chicken neck cast off the side of a small motorboat. Once a crab had taken her bait, she would pull it up with great suspense, losing more than she landed. Back at the house, she would spend the afternoon steaming and shelling and would have crab hors d'oeuvres ready in time for cocktail hour.

A crab boil takes the opposite approach: your guests do their share of the work (ideally outside on a picnic table that can be hosed down afterward), which is why it was always our go-to summer celebration. My brothers and I all had summer birthdays and would keep a running tally of how many crabs we could eat. Marrying a fellow Cancer and then giving birth to another means the tradition is here for good. Last year, we had our crab feast in arguably the best possible location for cleanup—the outdoor picnic table of a rented beach house—but tonight we are beached inland, setting up long folding tables on the roof. I am ready with extra bowls of melted butter to pass, a backup case of beer on ice, and a very long hose.

spicy crab and shrimp boil with corn and potatoes

The amount of crab and shrimp you need will depend on appetites and on how well your guests know each other. When you serve crabs in mixed company, even dear friends will shock you with their daintiness, but if it's a family dinner, as ours is tonight, you might expect people to put away eight or ten crabs apiece. If crabs aren't available, a seafood boil is equally delicious with just shrimp, especially if they are wild ones, still fresh enough to have their heads on.

SERVES 4 TO 8

Fill a 20-quart kettle (if using a smaller pot, do this in two or more batches) about one-quarter full with water and bring to a boil. Add a bottle of beer and season generously with salt, Old Bay seasoning, yellow or brown mustard seeds, coriander seeds, whole dried chiles, and a few bay leaves. Add a head of garlic, an onion, and a few lemons—all sliced in half. Simmer for about 15 minutes. Toss in 2 pounds small whole potatoes and return to a boil. Add about 2 dozen blue crabs, and cover the pot with a tight-fitting lid. When the crabs stop moving, about 4 minutes, sprinkle them with more Old Bay to taste. Add ears of shucked corn on top of the crabs, cover, and steam until it is nearly done, 4 to 5 minutes. Last, add 3 pounds fresh shrimp in their shells, seasoning them in the pot with salt and another generous sprinkling of Old Bay, and cover. When the shrimp are just pink and barely done, remove the pot from the heat and drain it. Cover a sturdy table with newspaper and pour the seafood, potatoes, and corn directly onto it. Pass bowls of melted butter, lemon wedges, more Old Bay, a few small mallets, crab crackers, and picks.

CHERRIES

Southern Virginia is not what most people in central North Carolina would consider local, but if you are talking about cherries, it's just up the road. Levering Orchard is a hundred-year-old fruit farm in the Blue Ridge mountains, home to forty-four varieties of cherries—sour, sweet, and everything in between. Family legend has it that founder Ralph Levering, a former strawberry farmer who tired of stooping down to pick his crops, walked from Asheville, North Carolina, to Roanoke, Virginia, and back, searching for the perfect spot to plant an orchard. Levering was mostly in apples until the early 1970s, when his son Sam took over and started replacing many of the apples with cherry trees, pushing the limits of what could be grown locally. The risk paid off: although Sam's son Frank Levering still grows apples—along with peaches, nectarines, and pears—he now has the largest cherry orchard in the region. People caravan there from all over the South after checking the cherry hotline for daily updates on ripening.

A year ago, Silvia, Monica, Phoebe, and Jenne picked almost two hundred pounds of cherries in a rollicking, bruising, and utterly competitive day of tree climbing and yellow-jacket swatting, returning to Lantern cherry-stained and way past dinnertime. Over cold beer and dumplings, they told their war stories, which were tolerated because we then got to eat cherries for months. The first few days, we were happy to just eat the fresh sweet cherries by the handful. Later in the week, I made a juicy cherry and red onion salad to go with grilled squab and Monica made cherry stone panna cotta, flavored by steeping the bitter almond–flavored cherry pits in the hot cream. Later still, we ate the cherries simmered in a wine bath, and then finally we ate the small sour cherries that we had candied to preserve them. Phoebe made double-crust pies for her favorite market customers and used the leftover juice to make cherry lemonade.

This year is turning out to be one of the worst on record for fruit. When Silvia and Monica returned to Levering this morning, they discovered that the orchard had lost almost its entire crop due to the recent rain; they returned with less than twenty pounds. But hedging her bets a few weeks ago, Monica had gotten some local sour cherries from Robert Tolbert, who has only a few trees but is just down the street. We pickled them in rice wine vinegar, sugar, and black pepper and are going to serve them with thin slices of an aged country ham that has been waiting for a special occasion.

squab with grilled red onion and sweet cherries

While the squab is resting, fry up the livers in a little butter in a small pan and season with salt. Mash them with a fork and flavor with a little gold rum to taste. Spread on grilled bread as a snack while you wait, or serve it alongside the squab.

SERVES 2

2 (1-pound) squabs
Juice of 1 lemon
4 tablespoons olive oil
Kosher salt and freshly ground black pepper
1 medium red onion
2½ teaspoons sugar
4 slices of rustic country bread
2 tablespoons good-quality red wine vinegar
About 16 sweet red cherries, pitted
10 fresh flat-leaf parsley leaves, torn
1 tablespoon unsalted butter, melted

Wash, dry, and trim the squabs. Remove the backbone from each with a large knife or poultry scissors. Lay the birds on a cutting board, breast side up. Crack the breastbone with one firm push of the palm of your hand to flatten out the bird. Rub the lemon juice and 1 tablespoon of the oil all over the birds and season liberally with salt and pepper. Marinate for an hour at room temperature or overnight in the refrigerator. If you refrigerate overnight, allow the birds to come to room temperature before cooking.

Prepare a hot fire in a charcoal grill.

Slice the onion into ½-inch-thick wedges, and keeping them as intact as possible, coat with 1 tablespoon of the oil, ½ teaspoon of the sugar, and salt and pepper to taste. When the grill is very hot, but the flame has died down and the coals are completely covered with ash, grill the onion slices on both sides until they have grill marks and are tender, 3 to 4 minutes.

Brush the bread slices with the remaining 2 tablespoons oil and grill for 2 to 3 minutes on each side, until marked.

Mix ¼ teaspoon salt with the remaining 2 teaspoons sugar and the vinegar in a medium bowl, stirring until the salt and sugar are dissolved. Add the cherries and allow them to marinate at room temperature. After the onions have cooled a little, add them to the cherries along with the parsley. Toss, and adjust the seasoning.

Push most of the coals to one side of the grill. Lay the marinated squabs, breast side up, on the half of the grill without the coals, arranging them so that they are as flat as possible. Grill for 8 to 10 minutes. Brush with the melted butter, then flip, and baste the grilled side with a little butter as well. Grill for another 8 to 10 minutes, until the legs are cooked through and the breast is about medium-rare. Be careful to avoid flare-ups and rotate the squabs (and if using a round kettle-style cooker, the grill itself) as necessary. Transfer the squabs to a warm platter and let them rest for 5 to 10 minutes. Arrange the cherry salad, grilled bread, and grilled squabs on plates.

the homeward angel

This variation on a Manhattan was created by longtime Lantern bar goddess Kristen Johnson and christened by Lantern lexicographer Phil Morrison. When naming his first novel, Thomas Wolfe is said to have been inspired by an engraving of a John Milton poem on a stone statue of an angel in a cemetery in Hendersonville, North Carolina, not too far from Levering Orchard:

Look homeward Angel now, and melt with ruth:

And, O ye Dolphins, waft the hapless youth.

SERVES I

2 ounces rye whiskey

½ ounce sweet vermouth

¼ ounce orange bitters

A splash of cherry pickling liquid (recipe follows)

2 Pickled Sour Cherries (recipe follows)

Pour the rye, vermouth, and bitters over ice in a cocktail mixer. Shake to chill before straining into a chilled glass. Add the cherry pickling liquid. Serve straight up, garnished with the pickled cherries.

pickled sour cherries

MAKES I QUART

1¼ cups rice vinegar

1 small slice of fresh ginger

15 black peppercorns

1¼ cups sugar

½ teaspoon kosher salt

4 cups pitted fresh sour cherries (about 1 pound)

In a small nonreactive saucepan, combine the vinegar, ginger, peppercorns, sugar, salt, and 1 cup water, and bring to a boil.

Put the cherries in a large heatproof jar and pour the hot vinegar mixture over them, covering them completely. When they have cooled, cover and refrigerate. These are best if they sit for at least a day before serving.

cherry stone panna cotta

This delicate, wobbling cream is perfumed with the mysterious cherry-almond essence contained in the kernel of the cherry pits—a reward for pitting the cherries.

SERVES 8

3 pounds cherries
2¼ cups heavy cream, or more if needed
1½ cups whole milk
¾ cup sugar
2¼ teaspoons unflavored powdered gelatin (1 envelope is 1 tablespoon)
¼ teaspoon kosher salt, or to taste

Pit the cherries, reserving ½ cup pits, and set the cherries aside for serving. Rinse the pits to remove any remaining fruit, and rub them in a clean tea towel to dry them. Now smash the pits: put them in another tea towel on a hard surface and smash them with a hammer so that they split open. Picking out just the kernels is tedious—it's fine to use the kernels and shells together.

Combine the pits, cream, milk, and sugar in a medium stainless-steel saucepan and bring to a boil. Stir, reduce the heat, and simmer for 10 to 12 minutes. (Like apple seeds, cherry pits contain very small amounts of cyanide, which is toxic only in relatively large quantities. However, heating the cherry pits will release fumes that you should not breathe in, so do this in a well-ventilated area and do not stick your head directly over the pan while the pits are simmering.) Remove from the heat, cover tightly, and set aside to steep for 1 hour.

Uncover the pan and return the liquid to a simmer. Meanwhile, put 2 tablespoons cold water in a medium bowl and sprinkle the gelatin over the water to allow it to soften. Let sit for 5 to 10 minutes.

Strain the hot liquid through a fine-mesh strainer into a measuring cup. You need 4 cups liquid total; add a little more cream if necessary. Slowly pour the hot cream mixture over the gelatin, whisking gently to dissolve the gelatin. Whisk in the salt and taste.

Set the bowl into an ice bath. Stir frequently so the panna cotta cools evenly. When it is slightly thickened, about 10 minutes, divide it among eight 4-ounce custard or tea cups. Cover the cups tightly with plastic wrap and refrigerate until set, 4 to 6 hours.

Serve in the cups or unmold if desired by gradually tipping the cup upside down above a plate while lifting one side of the panna cotta off the cup and easing it onto the plate. Serve with some of the fresh cherries.

CORN

Corn belongs on the cob, and if you run into it somewhere else, there had better be a good reason. Over the years, emancipated kernels have crept year-round into salad bars and risotto, floated sadly in otherwise normal bowls of soup, and sent pasta screaming to the Southwest. Good sweet corn does freeze well at home, but commercial niblets rarely taste like fresh summer corn and are not a substitute for the real thing.

Our window for unsprayed corn in the Piedmont is short—often just three weeks—and easily missed if you skip a few Saturday markets. I never get enough corn on the cob, and so it's usually only at the last second that I get around to making an actual corn recipe with fresh-off-the-cob kernels. Favorites include barely sautéed corn with fresh curry leaves and ghee or with black trumpet mushrooms and a little cream; made into a velvety soup; or fried into crispy corn "oysters"—fritters made with little else but corn and egg.

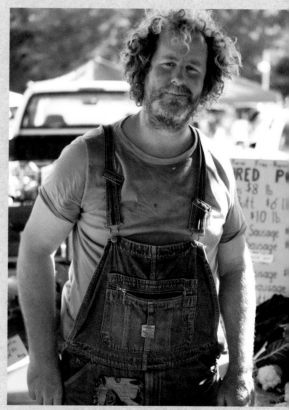

Eco Farm has the sweetest, juiciest corn at the Carrboro market, maybe because John and Cindy Soehner mainly grow it for their family to eat, saving just a bit for their customers. John has been known to hide his small crate of corn under his market table as an undeserving shopper approaches, or to test another with his deadpan promise of the lively corn earworm they will find at the top of each ear. A worm in every ear, virtually guaranteed in this part of the country for farmers who avoid pesticides, is a surprisingly easy sell for the funny, blunt former Long Island fisherman. But that worm is the devil you know, easily removed by trimming off the top 2 inches of the ear with a sharp knife before or after shucking.

crispy corn fritters

These are good as a savory side or drizzled with honey or sorghum for breakfast.

MAKES 30 SMALL FRITTERS

5 to 6 ears of corn, shucked
2 large eggs
Kosher salt
¾ cup all-purpose flour
½ teaspoon baking powder
⅛ teaspoon cayenne
Vegetable oil, for frying

On a large plate, using the coarse holes of a box grater, grate 5 ears of corn with swift downward strokes (to avoid the fiber from the cob). Be sure to catch all the milk. Measure the corn mixture, and if necessary continue with the last ear to make exactly 1 cup corn. Transfer it to a medium bowl.

Separate the eggs over a small bowl, allowing the whites to fall into the bowl and adding the yolks to the corn. With a fork, combine the yolks, corn, and ½ teaspoon salt. Sift the flour, baking powder, and cayenne directly onto the corn mixture and mix to combine.

Pour 2 inches of oil into a large, deep skillet, making sure that the oil does not fill the pan more than halfway, and heat over low heat. Meanwhile, beat the egg whites to soft peaks and gently fold them into the corn mixture. Raise the heat under the skillet to medium, and heat until the oil reaches 350°F on a deep-fat thermometer.

Working with two small tablespoons, carefully lay about 10 dollops of batter into the hot oil— fewer if they begin to crowd the pan. Fry for 2 to 3 minutes, until golden brown, flipping them about halfway through cooking. Transfer the fritters with a slotted spoon directly onto a clean brown paper bag to drain. Repeat with the remaining batter. Season with salt to taste, and serve immediately.

mexican corn on the cob

Elote—roasted corn on the cob spiked with salty cheese, creamy mayo, lime, and chile powder—is traditional Mexican street food, slightly exotic but homey enough to anyone who has scarfed roast corn at a state fair. It's also solid party food: guests can garnish their own, and because the pulled-down husk is used as a handle, it can easily be eaten standing up. Cotija cheese, widely available in supermarkets and Mexican *tiendas*, is a crumbly aged cow's-milk cheese, weirdly similar to both feta and Parmesan, and either can be substituted here.

Figure on 1 or 2 ears of corn per person. Gently pull back the husks from each ear of corn without detaching them, and remove as much of the silk as possible. Pull the husks back down to cover the corn, and then detach and discard the very outer layer of husks, leaving about a 2-husk-thick layer around each ear of corn. Put the corn in a large bowl or bucket, cover with cold water, and let soak for at least 30 minutes and up to 2 hours.

Prepare a charcoal grill.

Remove the corn from the water and give each ear a brisk shake. Grill the corn in its husk over very hot coals for 4 to 5 minutes, turning the corn occasionally, so that the husks get slightly charred all over and shrivel a little to expose some kernels. Continue to cook

for another 6 minutes or so, until some of the exposed kernels char a bit and the corn is tender. Peel back the husks and transfer the corn to a platter. Have guests first spread a thin layer of mayonnaise on the corn, followed by chile powder, grated Cotija, a squirt of lime, and salt to taste.

SCHLEPPING FOOD

We are getting ready for a week at the beach tonight, and as we start to load the car, Mac shoots me a look that says, "Can't we rough it for once?" By "roughing it" he means having to go grocery shopping and eat unripe tomatoes. But my goal for the week is to stay on the beach every night until dark and still get dinner ready before the kids are out of the bathtub. And anyway, it's too late; I already have everything I need: twenty-five pounds of tomatoes in all stages of ripeness, a chicken, five pounds of green and yellow wax beans, red torpedo onions, a slab of smoked bacon, a sack of cucumbers, a flat of eggs, lots of cheese—smoked farmer's, mozzarella, and aged goat—a few loaves of corn bread, links of dried sausage that can be served raw like a salami or added to clams, okra that will be fried alongside flounder, a watermelon, and a contentious number of zucchini and summer squashes.

I like to move food. The backseat of my car is always full of boxes and bags on their way to the restaurant or home from it: cured meat that will be hung in the cool basement, dried chiles or cellared potatoes and onions being taken back to be eaten, empty cartons to return to farms, and migrating bottles that I'll eventually refill with seltzer. Before Lantern opened, Phil pitched his favored name for the restaurant—"A Cup from Home"—referring not to a lovely phrase from a haiku, but to the perpetual china tea cup stationed next to my driver's seat.

Any trip worth making is also worth making with a few quarts of sauerkraut or a muffuletta. Last weekend, hearing that my brother's family in the Hudson Valley had had a tomato-less summer because of the blight, I squeezed a heavy box of nearly ripe ones into Mac's bag to take along on our visit, stopping to admire the big empty spot it would leave in the suitcase for the return trip. Fleisher's butcher shop in Kingston, New York, had the perfect things to fill it: a couple of smoked ham hocks and a beefy dry-aged sirloin, kept cool with a frozen 12-pack of home-made hot dogs.

At baggage claim, I can sometimes smell my suitcase before I see it: onion bagels, raw milk cheese, and pounds of fresh hard-neck garlic still with its papery stalks. During the height of mad-cow panic, I was stopped at the airport in Montreal trying to smuggle home a bag of Schwartz's smoked-meat sandwiches. Lesson: take at least a bite before entering security. And one of my best memories of our wedding weekend is the moment our friend Dave revealed that for my bachelorette party he had brought me a whole ham in his suitcase from Kurowycky's, the now shuttered Ukrainian smokehouse in Manhattan's East Village.

It took a few hours to load the car that night and we left some beach chairs and sea noodles in our wake. But when we finally got settled at the rental house, everyone had forgiven me for making them ride in a grocery cart. In the end, Mac was right that ten pounds of zucchini and squash was too much, and we really had to focus for those last few days to use them up. I needed the room in the car to bring back a few bushels of clams.

broiled baby zucchini with parmesan

SERVES 4 AS A SIDE DISH

1 pound (about 6) very small zucchini, roughly 1 inch in diameter
1 tablespoon olive oil
Kosher salt and freshly ground black pepper
1 cup coarsely grated Parmesan cheese

Preheat the oven to 475°F.

Wash and dry the zucchini, trimming the blossom and stem ends slightly if necessary. Quarter each zucchini lengthwise; if they are less than ¾ inch in diameter, cut them in half instead. In a medium bowl, toss the zucchini with the oil and season with salt and pepper. Lay them out on a baking sheet, end to end, cut sides up, in a tight row. Roast for about 8 minutes or until they are just starting to color but are still al dente, or half tender. Remove from the oven.

Preheat the broiler for several minutes until it is very hot. Sprinkle the zucchini with the cheese and broil until the cheese is golden brown and the zucchini are tender, 3 to 4 minutes.

grilled zucchini with mint, chile oil, and toasted pine nuts

SERVES 4

4 medium zucchini, sliced lengthwise ¼ inch thick
3 tablespoons extra virgin olive oil
Kosher salt
Chile Oil (page 141)
¼ cup pine nuts, lightly toasted
⅓ cup fresh mint leaves, torn into thin strips
2 heaping tablespoons shaved aged hard cheese, such as Vella Dry Jack or Parmesan
Freshly ground black pepper

Prepare a charcoal grill.

Brush each side of the zucchini slices with the oil and season generously with salt. When the grill is very hot, but the flame has died down and the coals are completely covered with ash, grill the zucchini on both sides until golden brown and just cooked through but still firm, 4 to 6 minutes. Arrange the zucchini slices on a serving platter and drizzle with chile oil. Sprinkle with the pine nuts, mint, cheese, and pepper.

zucchini "noodles" with ricotta

SERVES 2 AS A LIGHT MAIN COURSE

2 small tomatoes, cored and cut into small cubes

Kosher salt

3 medium zucchini

2 tablespoons extra virgin olive oil

2 large garlic cloves, very thinly sliced

1 small fresh hot red chile, split in half lengthwise to expose the seeds

Freshly ground black pepper

½ cup whole-milk ricotta cheese

1 cup mixed fresh tender herbs, such as basil, chives, and/or tarragon

3 tablespoons grated aged sheep's-milk cheese

Season the tomatoes with a little salt. Slice the zucchini lengthwise into long paper-thin slices, using a mandoline or a sharp vegetable peeler.

In a large sauté pan, heat the olive oil over low heat and sauté the garlic and chile until they are fragrant and softened but not browned, about 4 minutes. Season with a little salt. Add the zucchini, raise the heat to medium-high, and toss gently with tongs, seasoning very generously with salt and pepper. Continue to cook while tossing occasionally until the zucchini is slightly wilted and warmed through but still firm and not yet giving off very much liquid, about 2 minutes. Add the tomatoes and toss for a moment, until they are hot and begin to give off a little liquid. Reduce the heat to low and add the ricotta and herbs, combining them with the zucchini and tomatoes to create a creamy, light pink sauce. Divide between two warm bowls, and serve topped with the grated sheep's-milk cheese.

slow-cooked squash with butter and basil

SERVES 4 AS A SIDE DISH

2 tablespoons unsalted butter
1 small onion, diced
Kosher salt
4 cups ¾-inch cubed yellow crookneck squash (about 5 small to medium)
10 fresh basil leaves, torn into strips

Over very low heat, melt 1 tablespoon of the butter in a heavy saucepan. Add the onion and season with ½ teaspoon salt. Cover the pan with a tight-fitting lid and slowly sauté, stirring occasionally, for 6 to 8 minutes, until the onions are translucent and tender. If at any time the onions begin to brown, add a tablespoon of water.

Add the remaining 1 tablespoon butter and the squash, and season with 1 teaspoon salt. Cover and cook, stirring often, for 15 minutes, until the squash is just tender and beginning to fall apart but still has its bright yellow color. Add the basil and immediately stir it in to prevent the steam from turning it black. Cook, covered, for another couple of minutes, until the basil is wilted.

OLD BREEDS

Some of the best-tasting chicken we get in North Carolina comes via FedEx from Frank Reese in Kansas. Whenever I splurge and get some for Lantern, I make a big batch of fried chicken in a deep cast-iron skillet, slowly browning it in a few inches of rendered pork fat. Lard makes the best possible fried chicken and blissfully contains more of what is good for you and less of what is bad than most vegetable oils. It produces crisp, nutty, and nearly greaseless fried chicken that is of course perfect eaten hot but still remarkable at room temperature. Tonight we are having it for dinner with green beans with garlicky bread crumbs and a berry pudding. This weekend, I'll make some to take to a picnic, along with potato salad made with hard-boiled eggs and diced pickles, spiked with pickle juice.

I had never tasted real chicken—chicken bred and produced with flavor as the goal—until I met Frank Reese. His flock of Plymouth Barred Rocks is descended from the birds that his mother began raising in the 1930s and whose lineage dates back to the 1870s. A few years ago, in preparation for a blind tasting organized by the American Livestock Breeds Conservancy, Frank shipped us a box of his Plymouth Barred Rocks, along with a few of his Dark Cornish, a plump English variety used in the 1940s to breed the commercial Cornish Rock we are familiar with today. We tore into the FedEx box, seasoned two of the chickens with a little salt, dotted them with butter, and rushed them into the oven. The fragrance of these roasting birds caused a small commotion, and while they rested, we (our group had grown to include a deliveryman with a nose for lunch) gathered around the prep table for the carving. The Dark Cornish was small and fat, almost round in shape, and had cooked up a little deeper shade of golden brown. The Barred Rock looked a little skinny but was meaty at the prominent keel bone (the sloping bone that rises up in the center of the breast). Digging in, we agreed that they were the best bites of chicken any of us could remember—dense, nutty, and intensely chickeny. I took the bones home and made a stock so good that it had Oona demanding chicken soup for dinner for weeks.

All of us had eaten chicken from supermarkets and farmers' markets—chicken raised in tiny cages in factories and outdoors in pastures and in woods and all of the marketing classifications in between (indoor "barn-roaming," anyone?)—but none of us had ever tasted anything like these birds. Why? Because old breeds like the Plymouth Barred Rock and the Dark Cornish are slow-growing, taking as much as three to four months to develop. Almost all commercial chickens are Cornish Rocks, bio-engineered meat machines that grow at warp speed, from newly hatched chick to a three-pound shrink-wrapped dinner for four in as few as forty days. Even on the kindest farm, the Cornish Rock might be considered inhumane by definition—an animal born with a two-month expiration date, at which time many can no longer stand or maintain basic organ functions. Fast growth is lousy for the bird but even worse for its flavor and texture—its meat is cottony and soft from lack of movement and somehow dry no matter how perfectly cooked.

Frank's chickens, turkeys, and ducks, like Eliza MacLean's hogs (see page 20), are completely unique and no one tagline can capture why. His birds aren't certified organic and are local only if you live in Kansas. They are antibiotic- and hormone-free, air-chilled, and truly "natural" and "free-range"—but those don't completely get it either. With old breeds in vogue, it's relatively easy to find factory-raised "heritage" Berkshire pork intended to create the feeling of an on-farm dinner while hailing from a 5,000-hog operation. The complex, satisfying taste of old breeds is part of a bigger picture: putting taste before yield and profit, preserving ancient skills, caring for animals with compassion, and engaging a community of growers and eaters. What makes them delicious is their whole, complicated story. Raising old breeds the right way requires skill, time, and expense; a bird like

Frank's can cost as much as $25. But even so, a fried chicken picnic or Sunday dinner with mashed potatoes and gravy can still come in for not very much more per person than a take-out bucket.

fried chicken

SERVES 4

1 (3½- to 4-pound) chicken, rinsed, dried, trimmed, and cut into 10 pieces
2 cups buttermilk
2 tablespoons kosher salt
2 cups all-purpose flour
1½ teaspoons freshly ground black pepper
Lard or expeller-pressed vegetable oil, for frying

Put the chicken, buttermilk, and 1 tablespoon of the salt into a large bowl. Stir well and refrigerate overnight.

Drain the chicken in a colander and let it come to room temperature. Mix together the flour, remaining 1 tablespoon salt, and the pepper in a large bowl.

Put two large cast-iron skillets or other deep, heavy sauté pans on the stovetop and add lard to fill each about 1 inch deep. Heat over medium-high heat to 325°F. Starting with the dark meat, gently dredge one piece of the chicken in the flour mixture to coat it lightly. Avoid pressing the flour into the chicken; it should just be a dusting with any excess brushed off. As soon as a piece is floured, gently lay it in the hot oil and avoid the temptation to move it at all for the first few minutes, so that it doesn't stick. Repeat with the remaining dark meat and then move on to the white, ideally cooking the two in separate pans. Once a pan is about three-quarters full, reduce the heat to low and partially cover. Watch the chicken closely, turning the pieces with tongs as needed for even cooking and rotating the pan itself on the burner. As the first side turns deep golden brown, 8 to 10 minutes, turn the pieces over and continue to cook until they are evenly crisp and golden, another 8 to 10 minutes. Check for doneness; the dark meat will take a little longer than the white. Transfer the chicken to a clean brown paper bag to drain, and serve warm or at room temperature.

green beans with garlic bread crumbs and tomatoes

SERVES 4

½ small loaf of country white bread
1 medium ripe tomato, cored and chopped into ½-inch cubes
Kosher salt
2 tablespoons olive oil
1 pound green beans, trimmed
Freshly ground black pepper
2 garlic cloves, minced

Preheat the oven to 250°F.

Remove the crust from the bread, tear the bread into 2- to 3-inch chunks, and scatter them on a baking sheet. Bake for 15 minutes until the outside is firm and crusty but not browned and the inside is still soft. Let the bread cool.

Meanwhile, toss the chopped tomatoes with ¼ teaspoon salt and 1 tablespoon of the oil, and set aside.

Bring a large pot of salted water to a boil.

Tear the cooled bread into ¼- to ½-inch pieces. Measure out 1 cup and reserve the rest for another use. Put the bread crumbs in a small skillet and toast over medium-high heat for 4 to 6 minutes, until golden. Transfer to a plate and set aside.

Blanch the green beans in the boiling water for 3 to 5 minutes, until just tender. Drain and transfer to a warm serving dish. Add the tomatoes and toss, seasoning with a little salt and pepper.

Heat the remaining 1 tablespoon oil in the same small skillet over medium heat, and add the garlic. Sauté just until it begins to turn golden and is fragrant, about 30 seconds. Quickly add the bread crumbs and toss to combine. Sprinkle over the beans.

chilled berry pudding with cream

SERVES 8

1 loaf of white sandwich bread (12 to 14 slices), crusts removed, left out on a rack overnight

5 pints very ripe mixed berries, such as blueberries, blackberries, raspberries, and/or hulled strawberries cut into small wedges

½ cup sugar, or a little more if the berries are not very sweet

¾ teaspoon kosher salt

Juice of ½ lemon

Vegetable oil, for greasing the pan

Heavy cream, cold, for serving

Trim the slices of bread to fit snugly in an ideally straight-sided 9 × 5-inch loaf pan (there will be enough for three layers), and set them aside.

Combine the berries, sugar, and salt in a large nonreactive saucepan and heat over medium-low heat. Stir well and bring to a simmer. Reduce the heat, stir again, and cook for 1 minute, until the sugar is just dissolved and the berries have begun to release their juices but are not cooked. Let cool slightly and then add the lemon juice. Strain the berry juice into a bowl and set both the berries and the juice aside.

Lightly grease the loaf pan and line it with plastic wrap, leaving enough wrap on the ends to cover the pudding later. Spoon one third of the berries into the pan in an even layer. Dip a few slices of the bread into the berry juice and arrange them to cover the bottom of the pan completely. Spoon another third of the berries onto the bread. Repeat the process, finishing with a layer of bread on top. Pour the remaining berry juice over the pudding. Fold the plastic wrap snugly over the top and cover with a piece of cardboard, trimmed to fit inside the pan. Weight it with a few cans or a brick wrapped in foil, set it on a plate to catch any drips, and refrigerate overnight or for up to 2 days.

To serve, unmold the pudding onto a serving platter, and slice. Serve with a pitcher of cold cream for pouring on top.

EGGPLANT AND OKRA

Free food rouses courage. That is where I was coming from the first time I cooked eggplant; I had bought a bag for next to nothing from the vegetable stand across the street from my first apartment. I came home and discovered a miraculous Pierre Franey recipe: soft butter seasoned with grated Parmesan cheese and parsley and spread on thick rounds of eggplant and broiled until tender and golden—and ate it like that for days.

The suggestion to salt eggplant is common, but I have never found it necessary for any but the largest and seediest cases. The best eggplants are shiny with tight skin, small for their type, and heavy for their size. Since it will absorb huge amounts of oil if you encourage it, one good strategy is blackening the whole eggplant directly on an open gas flame and then peeling as with roasted peppers (see page 117). Another good alternative to sautéing on the stovetop is roasting eggplant in a 450°F oven. At Lantern, we use mostly skinny purple-black Japanese eggplants, slicing them thick on the bias, tossing in a light coating of oil, seasoning with salt and pepper, and then throwing them onto a preheated scorching-hot baking sheet and into the oven, flipping them once while they roast. The result is tender, caramelized, and not at all greasy eggplant that can then be sauced in many ways. We often dress it with garlicky Asian chile paste, lime, and honey; a little garlic oil tossed with tender herbs is good, too.

Like eggplant, okra responds well to high heat and dry-ish cooking styles. I like to roast the pods whole in a very hot oven, then toss them with chiles and a squeeze of lime. Or I cut them into thick diagonal slices and "dry-fry" them with just a bare minimum of oil and finish them with aromatics like minced ginger and brown mustard seeds and just enough diced raw tomato to create a sauce. I love deep-fried okra too; I slice it thin and toss it in chickpea flour before its hot-oil plunge.

Late this morning at a farmers' market tasting, I managed to cook both of these divisive vegetables—together at last—for a hungry crowd. I found that if you (loudly) dislike one, you may also have (even louder) feelings about the other—and the loudest of all have never tried either. But free food is persuasive and we were all out before lunchtime.

eggplant salad
with walnuts and garlic

Steaming eggplant gives it a suave, custardy texture that helps it resist soaking up too much oil, setting it up for this rich dressing. I like Anaheim chile flakes here, which are milder than the standard-issue chile flakes. They provide sweet pepper flavor without too much heat.

SERVES 4 AS A SIDE DISH

8 small Japanese eggplants, about 6 inches long and 1 inch across
2 garlic cloves, crushed
1 teaspoon kosher salt
Juice of 1 lemon
¼ cup olive oil
1 teaspoon mild Anaheim chile flakes, less if using regular chile flakes
¾ cup walnuts, lightly toasted and any loose skin rubbed off
¼ cup coarsely chopped fresh flat-leaf parsley

Cut each eggplant in half crosswise into 3-inch-thick rounds and then quarter them lengthwise. In a vegetable steamer over medium-high heat, and in batches if necessary, steam the eggplant for 10 to 12 minutes, until it is tender but not yet falling apart. Let the eggplant cool on a plate, discarding any liquid that accumulates.

Mash the garlic and salt together into a smooth paste, using the side of a knife. Transfer the paste to a medium bowl and stir in the lemon juice, olive oil, and chile flakes. Coarsely chop the walnuts and add them. Add the parsley and eggplant, and mix well.

fried okra with indian spices and hot tomato relish

SERVES 4 AS A SMALL APPETIZER

1 teaspoon coriander seeds
¼ teaspoon fennel seeds
1 clove
1 teaspoon cumin seeds
Vegetable oil, for frying
1 large egg
¼ cup buttermilk
1 medium serrano chile, finely chopped
2 tablespoons chickpea flour
2 tablespoons all-purpose flour
½ teaspoon kosher salt
½ teaspoon freshly ground black pepper
2 pints okra (just under a pound), stems removed
Sea salt, for serving
Hot Tomato Relish (recipe follows)

In a small pan over medium heat, lightly toast the coriander, fennel, and clove until fragrant, 1 to 2 minutes. Allow to cool completely; then grind and set aside. Toast the cumin seeds in the same fashion and add them to the ground spices.

Fill a deep, heavy stockpot with about 3 inches of oil. Heat the oil over medium-high heat until a deep-fat thermometer reads 350°F.

Beat the egg in a small bowl and whisk in the buttermilk and serrano chile. In a medium bowl, combine the chickpea flour, all-purpose flour, salt, pepper, and spice mixture.

Cut the okra on a sharp diagonal into long ¼-inch-thick slices. Put the okra slices into the bowl with the flour mixture and combine, leaving a light dusting on each piece. Pour the egg mixture on top and mix with your hands, making sure to coat all surfaces. In batches, use a large slotted spoon to carefully lay loosely formed handfuls of 6 to 8 slices into the hot oil and cook for about 2 minutes, turning as necessary until the okra is golden brown and uniformly crisp. Drain on a clean brown paper bag, season with sea salt, and serve with the tomato relish.

hot tomato relish

This keeps for several weeks in the fridge and is good with spiced basmati rice, grilled chicken or lamb, or a creamy corn stew.

MAKES 2 CUPS

1 tablespoon expeller-pressed vegetable oil
½ teaspoon brown mustard seeds
3 garlic cloves, slivered lengthwise
½ teaspoon cayenne
1¼ teaspoons ground turmeric
5 ripe plum tomatoes, peeled, seeded, and finely diced
½ teaspoon kosher salt
¼ cup distilled white vinegar
¼ teaspoon sugar

Heat the oil in a medium-size heavy nonreactive pot over medium-high heat. Add the mustard seeds and garlic, and cook until the garlic is turning light golden brown and the seeds are popping, about 2 minutes. Add the cayenne and turmeric. Cook for 10 to 20 seconds, and then add the tomatoes, salt, vinegar, and sugar. Simmer for 15 minutes, or until the tomatoes are soft and the relish has thickened slightly. Serve hot.

TOMATO MAINTENANCE

The secret to eating great tomatoes all summer long lies not in which variety you plant or what stand you buy from, but in watching them—making space for them to lie flat someplace cool near the kitchen, checking them daily, eating the ones that need eating, and continuously making plans for the ones that are getting there. Even tomatoes that are picked ripe need a little time out at room temperature to reach their peak flavor. It is shocking how long it can take even a just slightly firm tomato to get there . . . and how fast a perfect one rots. At the restaurant we have huge sheet pans, baskets, and boxes of tomatoes occupying every free spot, from the top of the office printer to underneath the china cabinets. Tomato maintenance is on our daily summer prep list. When I checked them this morning, I designated the ripe and juicy ones for tomato salad tonight, dangerously ripe ones for a spicy tomato relish this afternoon, and small firm cherry tomatoes for pickling to serve with basil in a spicy vodka cocktail. My personal payoff was a few pounds of super-ripe "uglies" that made a rich, spicy tomato juice that will spike our kitchen beers at the end of service tonight. In summer, tomato maintenance is usually the first thing that we train a new hire to do: if she or he doesn't get it—the cultivated OCD that it takes to do the job well—then we know that person won't work out.

All that said, the ultimate tomato is one that was not only well maintained but also bred for flavor at the table. Our family favorite in New Jersey in the 1970s was the hybrid Ramapo, developed at Rutgers University in 1968. Deeply flavorful but resistant to cracking and disease, it was considered too soft to ship and fell out of favor but is happily making a comeback. Some of my favorite heirlooms include complex Cherokee Purples, low-yield intense Brandywines, dusky purple-black cherries, bright acidic Green Zebras (which stay green when ripe), meaty orange Kellogg's Breakfasts, huge Mortgage Lifters (perfect for tomato sandwiches), and sweet fuzzy Garden Peaches.

tomato sandwich

Alex and Betsy Hitt were among the first farmers to sell heirloom tomatoes at the Carrboro farmers' market almost thirty years ago, and each summer in mid-June they post a sign above their stand that reads: "Get your bread and mayonnaise ready—the tomato flood is coming!" A tomato sandwich–thick slices of dead-ripe tomatoes well seasoned with salt and pepper between slices of soft white sandwich bread spread with rich mayonnaise—is pure joy. Any attempt to "improve" it—toasting the bread, adding lettuce or, god forbid, basil—will only distract from perfection.

AL KUFFA

DR. WHYCHEES

ANESE
ACK
RIFELE

GERMAN
JOHNSO

GREE
ZEBR

BRANDY
WINE

TESS' LAND
RACE CURRANT

ANNAS NOIR

A
GE

FLAMINGO

PERSIMMON

BIG ZEBRA

BLACK
KRIM

CHOCOLATE
CHERRY

CHERRY

RISENSTRAUBE

YELLOW
PEAR

ISIS
CANDY

SUNGOLD

MULE
TEAM

kathe's baked plum tomatoes with olive oil and bread crumbs

My mom makes these delicious baked tomatoes as an entrée in a vegetable-plate dinner or as a side dish for grilled meat. Make a double batch of the seasoned crumbs, if you'd like; they freeze very well and can be used with equally good results on many summer vegetables.

SERVES 4 AS A SIDE DISH

4 tablespoons olive oil
12 very ripe plum tomatoes, cut in half lengthwise and seeded
Kosher salt and freshly ground black pepper
¾ cup fine, very lightly toasted bread crumbs (recipe follows)
⅓ cup finely grated Parmesan or other hard, flavorful aged cheese such as Vella Dry Jack
⅓ cup finely chopped fresh herbs such as parsley, tarragon, basil, chives, and/or mint
1 small garlic clove, mashed to a paste
1 small shallot, finely chopped

Preheat the oven to 325°F.

Coat a shallow baking dish with 1 tablespoon of the oil. Arrange the halved tomatoes, cut side up, snugly in the dish and season with ½ teaspoon salt and some pepper.

In a small bowl, drizzle the bread crumbs with 2 tablespoons of the oil and combine with the Parmesan, herbs, garlic, shallot, ¼ teaspoon salt, and pepper to taste. Top each tomato half with about a tablespoon of the bread crumb mixture. Drizzle the remaining 1 tablespoon oil over the tomatoes, and bake for 45 to 60 minutes, until they are tender and slightly shrunken and the bread crumbs are golden brown. The riper the tomatoes, the shorter the cooking time will be.

fine lightly toasted bread crumbs

MAKES ABOUT 2 CUPS

1 small loaf of country bread

Preheat the oven to 300°F.

Remove the crust and cut the bread into roughly 1-inch cubes. Spread them out on a baking sheet and bake, tossing them once or twice, until they are crispy and dry but without much color, 25 to 30 minutes. Let cool completely. Then grind, in batches, in a spice mill until fine. Keeps frozen for several months.

tomato juice

This is a good idea for an abundance of tomatoes that are threatening to rot. The juice keeps refrigerated for several days and can be frozen for up to 6 months.

MAKES ABOUT 6 CUPS

5 pounds very ripe tomatoes, cored and cut into chunks
1 tablespoon kosher salt
2 teaspoons black peppercorns
1 celery stalk
1 medium yellow onion, halved

Put the tomatoes and accumulated juices in a nonreactive pot and add the salt, peppercorns, celery, and onion. Bring to a simmer over low heat, cover, and cook for 15 minutes. Let cool.

Discard the celery and onion, and then strain through a fine-mesh sieve, using a rubber spatula to push the tomatoes through. Discard the solids.

michelada

SERVES 2

Kosher salt, for rimming the glasses
1 lime, quartered
½ cup Tomato Juice (above)
Hot sauce
1 Mexican beer, such as Bohemia, cold

Pour enough salt on a small plate to cover it. Rub the rims of two glasses with lime wedges and then dip each glass in the salt to coat the rims. To each glass add ¼ cup tomato juice, a dash of hot sauce, and a few ice cubes. Squeeze a lime wedge into each glass and discard. Slowly pour in the beer, dividing it between the two glasses, and garnish with the remaining lime wedges.

PEPPERS

Peppers are among the last summer vegetables on the scene; some arrive so late in August and early September that they can seem more like a fall crop than a summer one. Many of my favorite ways to deal with heat-loving peppers involve preserving them for use in the fall and beyond—salting or pickling spicy chiles (page 141) or blackening bell peppers directly on the stovetop, peeling, and slicing them and then covering them with oil. I'll puree some of the roasted peppers into a paste that can be stored in the freezer and then in cold months spread on a flatbread along with a soft cheese or stirred into stewed rice at the end of cooking. During the rest of the year, there is no point in spending the time and money roasting watery hothouse bell peppers, which are expensive and flavorless. The rich, dusky scarlet bell peppers I got yesterday from Bill Dow of Ayrshire Farm are so ripe that they are just starting to shrink slightly; even raw they are almost more jammy than crunchy.

marinated roasted peppers in a jar

When red bell peppers are best (and least expensive) in the late summer and early fall, this is a good dish to make in a big batch.

Turn one or more gas burners to high and place the whole peppers directly on the burners. As they char, turn them with tongs so that the entire surface of the pepper becomes completely papery and blackened. As they are finished, place the peppers in a paper bag. (If you don't have gas burners or a well-ventilated kitchen, cut the peppers in half lengthwise, put them on a baking sheet, cut side down, and broil them instead.)

When the peppers are cool enough to handle, peel and seed them. Slice them thick and toss them with olive oil, salt, and a few smashed and peeled garlic cloves. Put the peppers in a large wide-mouthed jar and top off with olive oil to cover by an inch. Refrigerate for at least several hours and up to a week.

flash-fried shishito peppers with sea salt

The spice level of both shishitos and the fleshier *pimiento de padrón* are unpredictable—most have a gentle zip, while the occasional pepper, about one in seven, is quite hot, adding some drama to cocktail time.

SERVES 4 AS AN APPETIZER

Expeller-pressed vegetable oil, for frying
1 pound fresh shishito or padrón peppers
Flaky sea salt, such as Maldon

Fill a deep heavy pot with 3 to 4 inches of oil. The oil should not fill the pot by more than one third. Heat the oil over medium heat until a deep-fat thermometer reads 350°F. Add a big handful or two of peppers to the oil and immediately cover the pot with a lid to avoid splattering. After about 10 seconds, carefully remove the lid and give the peppers a quick stir. Continue to cook with the lid off for another 10 seconds or so, until the peppers are blistered and beginning to color. Remove from the oil and drain on a clean paper paper bag. Transfer to a serving platter and sprinkle generously with salt. Serve them fresh and hot as you continue to cook more.

KILLING CRABS

My mom is here tonight and I'm cooking soft-shell crabs. It's a dinner version of a clichéd gift for Mom: something she loves but would never get for herself. Everything can be done in advance, except for the last-minute frying—I put together the ingredients for a crisp cucumber salad earlier this afternoon, kept them cold, and tossed them all together just before dinner.

Blue crabs caught just before they shed their hard shells are called peelers. Once they molt, they are softshells: 100 percent savory meat, eaten with the new paper-thin shell and all. In North Carolina, and the season starts in early May when the water first warms up, the prices are very high as almost all our crabs head to New York City or Washington, D.C. The season can extend as late as mid-fall, but by then crabs are so scarce that it is less about what you are willing to pay and more about who you know. With crab catches on the decline and the price for softshells many times higher than hardshells, watermen increasingly specialize in peelers, catching them by baiting their pots with live jimmies—male crabs that attract the she-crabs who are ready to molt and then mate. A waterman can have hundreds of "jimmy-pots," which in high season need to be checked every day—exhausting, monotonous work. After being transferred to a shedding tank where they are monitored 24/7 until the females molt, they are packed in shallow boxes lined with eelgrass and rushed to market alive. So when you splurge for fresh softshells, the work is mostly done, except for that one small detail: dressing them.

Tonight I kept them very cold so that they stayed drowsy and killed them so quickly and silently that the kids, who were playing on the kitchen floor, never even looked up. To kill or "clean" them, snip off the front ½ inch of the crab in a straight line just behind its eyes with a sharp kitchen knife. Lift the pointed corners on each side of the crab and remove and discard the spongy gills. If you wish, also remove the yellow "mustard," or tomalley (the hepatopancreas gland, which functions much like a liver, filtering impurities), now, too. Flip the crab over on its back and pull off the flap, or "apron," that is tucked in close against the belly. Try to avoid rinsing the crab; instead just gently pat it dry inside and out with a paper towel. Carefully lay each crab in one layer on a tea towel—once cleaned, crabs are even more fragile than when alive. Even though it's ideal to prepare them as close to cooking time as possible, I usually try to take care of it early enough to sip a glass of wine and create a little space between the killing and the eating.

The perfect softshell is crunchy, tender, and juicy all at once. Achieving that state is more a function of how the crabs were treated before you bought them than exactly how you cook them: only buy crabs that are alive and firm, with claws that feel full rather than limp and wrinkled. When you have crabs that are just right, a light coating of flour seasoned with salt and pepper and pan-fried in clarified butter is all that is needed. A more assertive dredge of rice flour spiced with garlic and black pepper creates a slightly crispier crab that is still delicate enough for Mom.

garlic and black pepper soft-shell crabs

SERVES 4

Vegetable oil, for frying
3 cups rice flour
1 tablespoon kosher salt
¼ cup freshly ground black pepper
¼ cup minced garlic
½ cup fish sauce
8 large soft-shell crabs, preferably jumbo or "whale" size, dressed and cut in half crosswise

Fill a deep, heavy pot with a lid about one-third full with oil, and heat it until a deep-fat thermometer reads 375°F.

In the meantime, combine the rice flour, salt, pepper, and garlic in a medium bowl. Put the fish sauce in a small bowl. Dip each piece of crab very briefly into the fish sauce, gently shaking off excess, and then into the rice flour mix. Roll the crab over and shake off any extra flour. Set aside. Repeat this process, until all the crab halves are dredged.

When the oil reaches 375°F, gently lay the crabs, top side down, in the oil. Don't crowd the pot—if necessary, fry them in batches—and use the lid as needed when the crabs are first added to the oil to avoid splattering. After 1 to 2 minutes, when the crabs are golden brown, turn them over and cook for another 2 minutes. Drain on clean brown paper bags and eat hot.

cucumber salad with lemon basil

SERVES 4 TO 6

¼ cup fresh lime juice (2 limes)

2 teaspoons kosher salt

2 tablespoons fish sauce

1 tablespoon sugar

1 tablespoon expeller-pressed vegetable oil

3 medium cucumbers (about 1½ pounds), thinly sliced

2 teaspoons finely chopped fresh red Thai chiles

1 cup thinly sliced scallions, white and green parts

¼ cup lemon basil, other basil, or mint leaves, torn

In a medium bowl, whisk together the lime juice, salt, fish sauce, sugar, and oil. Add the cucumbers and chiles, toss to combine, and let sit in the refrigerator for at least 10 and up to 30 minutes. Just before serving, add the scallions and basil. Toss again, and adjust the seasoning if necessary.

watermelon jell-o with gin

SERVES 6

½ medium watermelon
1 tablespoon (1 packet) unflavored powdered gelatin
3 tablespoons sugar, or more to taste
½ teaspoon kosher salt
⅓ cup good-quality gin
3 tablespoons fresh lemon juice, or a little more to taste
Toasted Watermelon Seeds (recipe follows)

Slice off the peel of the melon and cut the flesh into 2-inch chunks, removing as many seeds as possible and reserving them. You should have about 8 cups. Process the watermelon chunks in a blender until smooth. Place the puree in a paper coffee filter set in a strainer or sieve set over a bowl, and allow it to strain without pushing it through, about 15 minutes. You'll need exactly 3 cups juice; measure that out and drink any that remains.

Pour 1 cup of the watermelon juice into a medium bowl, sprinkle it with the gelatin, and allow the gelatin to soften for 10 minutes.

In a small nonreactive saucepan, heat 1 cup of the juice until it is just hot. Remove it from the heat and add the sugar, stirring to dissolve. Add the hot juice to the gelatin mixture and stir until the gelatin is completely dissolved. Add the remaining 1 cup juice, the salt, the gin, and the lemon juice. Taste the mixture to make sure the flavors are balanced. The sweetness and acidity of watermelons will vary, and if necessary gradually adjust with additional sugar and/or lemon juice.

Strain the mixture through a fine-mesh sieve into another bowl, and place it in an ice bath. Let it cool for 5 to 7 minutes, giving it a gentle stir with a spoon (rather than a whisk to avoid bubbles) several times. The gelatin will have started to thicken and become syrupy. Divide the mixture among six 5-ounce glasses. Chill in the refrigerator until completely set, at least 4 hours or overnight.

Garnish with toasted watermelon seeds, if desired, before serving.

toasted watermelon seeds

Rinse the watermelon seeds and pat them dry with a paper towel. Toss with a little oil and a generous sprinkling of salt. Roast on a baking sheet in a preheated 350°F oven, stirring occasionally, until they are very crunchy, about 15 minutes. Let cool.

SHELLING PARTY

Drinking beer in broad daylight feels totally productive when you are sitting outside in the yard at a big table shelling field peas, especially when that's what's for dinner.

Southern field peas are beans, only loosely related to garden peas. Thought to have been among the first cultivated crops—originating in West Africa and traveling far and wide before reaching North America via slave ships in the 1600s—they quickly became an essential southern food. Many dozens of varieties are grown across the South. Their names and how they are categorized vary, contradict, and overlap by region, but every pea has its own distinct flavor and story: For example, washday cooks up quickly after a long day of housework, and the red and white–speckled Ham and Gravy creates its own earthy sauce. There are also luscious butter beans, which are small, tender limas, more closely related to green beans than field peas; delicate cream or "lady" peas, like White Acre; meaty, nearly square crowder peas ("crowded" into their bursting pods); zippers, referring to how easily they can be shelled; pink-eyed purple-hull peas; deep purple pod and chartreuse peas with a blushing lavender eye; and the rich brown Dixie Lee.

The harvest begins here in mid to late summer, when the pods are plump with beans and begin to dry. Early on, fresh field peas and beans need only a brief simmer in a little salty water to become tender; cooked this way, small limas brighten a snack of ham and sheep's-milk cheese or tender purple-hull peas lend an appealing creamy, nutty texture to marinated sliced ripe tomatoes. Most blanched fresh field peas and beans are terrific as a fresh bean salad, marinated with olive oil and lemon, or further cooked by braising with sautéed aromatics like onions, carrots, and fennel. From there, raw diced tomatoes or a pounded aromatic herb like mint or basil can be added to the braised beans for a side dish/sauce in one for grilled fish or poultry. As the harvest continues and the peas get meatier, they are good stewed with ham bones or dried mushrooms.

As the season winds down, some peas are left out in the fields to dry on the vine, then are harvested and stored for cold-weather meals. Dried peas are tasty and versatile, but when I have the chance, I like to freeze the fresh ones; they retain more of their character and are less starchy than dried. To freeze, spread shelled peas or beans in a shallow layer on a small baking sheet and place in the freezer. Once frozen, transfer them to zip-top bags.

COOKING FIELD PEAS

Cooking times for field peas—whether fresh, frozen, or dried—vary greatly. In general, the smaller and fresher, the faster they cook. Peas can take as little as 5 to 10 minutes if tiny (even straight from the freezer), 20 to 45 minutes if bigger, and up to an hour or longer if dried. The key is to cook them in a flavorful, well-seasoned liquid and to check for doneness frequently, adjusting the amount of liquid with water as needed to create the right amount of brothiness for the dish.

warm edamame with seven-spice powder

While field peas date back to colonial times, edamame—fresh, young soybeans bred for human consumption, not animal feed—are relatively new to North Carolina, recently promoted to farmers here as a new crop to help replace tobacco. They make a good appetizer for a pea-shelling party since you can actually eat them on the side while shelling the peas for the main course.

SERVES 4

4 cups fresh or frozen edamame in pods
1 to 2 tablespoons Seven-Spice Powder (recipe follows), to taste
Flaky sea salt, such as Maldon

In a large pot of boiling salted water, blanch the edamame for 4 to 7 minutes, until tender. Drain in a colander. Transfer to a bowl and toss with the spice powder and some salt.

seven-spice powder

Leftover spice powder can be stored in an airtight container for a few weeks and makes a surprising addition to noodles, soups, and sashimi.

MAKES ABOUT 1 CUP

1 tablespoon white sesame seeds, toasted
1 tablespoon black sesame seeds, toasted
2 tablespoons plus 1 teaspoon fine Korean chile powder or finely ground flakes from
    a semi-hot dried chile, such as Ancho
2½ teaspoons poppy seeds
2½ teaspoons sansho powder (optional)
1½ teaspoons kosher salt
¼ sheet of nori, finely chopped
Grated zest of 1 small orange

Mix all of the ingredients together in a bowl.

Note: Sansho, which is made from the ground berries of the prickly ash tree and is related to Sichuan pepper, has a similarly numbing heat, but with bright lemony notes.

BACKYARD FRUIT

I got a wispy twig of a fig tree for my birthday from Jenne and Phoebe the summer that Oona was born. We stuck it in the ground and forgot about it, and the very next year, the tree—a Celeste, a rare variety here among the more common Brown Turkey—bore an impressive amount of small, sweet fruit with khaki skin and deep pink hearts. With no kindness from us and several years of drought, it's now so big that Oona swings from its branches and climbs high to pick. Fig trees grow like weeds in this town, but you still can't order figs from a produce company and they are even hard to come by at the farmers' market. If you want a steady supply of fresh figs, you need to have a tree or know someone who does. Friends come to the back door of restaurants with small pint boxes or egg cartons full, more a gift than an exchange, since no one could pay the real value of what the fruit represents: the rusty ladder, the fight with the birds, the disappointment of off-years. The ancient Greeks were forbidden from exporting figs, which they considered a common good. That is the argument that otherwise law-abiding fig lovers here make as they wander their neighborhoods late at night, eating as they go yard to yard, tree to tree.

They have justification; it's rare to see properly ripe and delicious figs in a restaurant because they need to be picked that way and start to go downhill soon after. When truly ripe, they are very soft and store best in a single layer in the refrigerator with a tea towel tucked on top. Today I woke to a fig emergency: three full quarts approaching overripeness. I immediately e-mailed expert gardener and food preserver Edith Calhoun for her pickled fig recipe.

edith calhoun's pickled figs

MAKES 6 CUPS

2 cups cider vinegar
4 cups sugar
2½ teaspoons kosher salt
½ teaspoon allspice berries
1 teaspoon cloves
3 pounds small fresh figs, ripe but firm with stems

In a medium nonreactive pot, bring the vinegar, 3 cups of the sugar, and the salt to a simmer. Add the allspice and cloves and let steep off the heat for 10 minutes. Add the figs to the pot, return to a simmer, and cook over low heat for 10 minutes. Let cool and then refrigerate overnight.

The next day, bring the figs back to a simmer with the remaining 1 cup sugar over low heat and cook for 10 minutes until they are soft, slightly shrunken, and flavorful. Allow the figs to cool before refrigerating, where they will keep for a month or so.

broiled ripe figs
with warm ricotta and honey

SERVES 2

1 cup fresh whole-milk ricotta
2 teaspoons honey, plus more for drizzling
¼ teaspoon kosher salt
¼ cup turbinado sugar
8 large ripe figs, with stems, cut in half lengthwise

Preheat the broiler, setting the rack as high as possible.

In a small bowl, combine the ricotta, honey, and salt.

Sprinkle the sugar on a small plate and dip each fig half, cut side down, into it, coating the entire surface with a thin, even layer. Place the figs, sugar side up, on a baking sheet and place it under the broiler. Broil for 4 to 6 minutes, or until all the sugar is completely melted and dark brown. Watch closely!

Serve with the ricotta mixture and an additional drizzle of honey.

ICEBOX PICKLES AND MORE

The real me never cans, but the acquisitive me continues to buy every jar lifter or pickle poker that falls in my path, so I have a drawer full of virgin canning gear. In actual fact, preserving food takes no special equipment at all—just the food itself and salt and/or sugar, some vinegar, and an hour or two. Most preserved foods, like pickles, jams, flavored oils, and salt-cured food, keep perfectly in the refrigerator for a long time—in many cases a very long time. If you have ever had a jar of jam or dill pickles open in the fridge for more than a week or two, you get my point. While pickling slows time, it doesn't suspend it; in the deli's pickle barrel, today's half-sours are next week's full-sours. All pickles—whether made with vinegar (like classic bread and butters) or brined and fermented (as with dill pickles, sauerkraut, or kimchi)—are in progress until you eat them. The vinegared ones get stronger and the brined ones tangier and softer.

pickled carrots and fennel with dill and coriander

MAKES 5 QUARTS

¼ cup kosher salt

10 black peppercorns

10 coriander seeds

1 head of garlic, unpeeled, cut in half crosswise

3 quarts (about 2 pounds) small baby carrots, any stems trimmed to ½ inch

5 small fennel bulbs, trimmed, fronds reserved, sliced lengthwise ⅓ inch thick

5 sprigs fresh dill

3 fresh New Mexico (Anaheim) chiles, sliced, seeds left intact

In a small saucepan over high heat, bring 2 cups water to a boil. Remove from the heat and add the salt, peppercorns, coriander, and garlic. Let cool and then add the mixture to 2 quarts cold water.

Layer the carrots, fennel, dill, and chiles in a crock or a large glass jar. Pour the brine over the vegetables, covering them completely. Put a small plate on top so that it keeps everything submerged. Store in a cool (65° to 70°F is ideal), dark room for about a week, checking every day or so and skimming off any mold or foam that rises to the top. The pickles are done when they are pleasantly sour and tangy but still firm. Refrigerate for up to 3 weeks.

pickled pumpkin

Use small organic pumpkins or squashes. Before peeling, taste their skins. If they are very tender, they can be left on. Pickled pumpkin is good served with crispy roast pork seasoned with five-spice or on its own as part of a pickle plate.

MAKES 2 QUARTS

2 cups rice vinegar
¾ cup distilled white vinegar
¾ cup mirin
5 fresh Thai chiles, split in half lengthwise
1 small piece of ginger, unpeeled, thinly sliced
6 garlic cloves
10 white peppercorns
1¼ cups sugar
¼ cup kosher salt
3 pounds pumpkin, cut into thin moons or chunks

Combine 2 cups water, the vinegars, mirin, chiles, ginger, garlic, peppercorns, sugar, and salt in a large nonreactive pot and bring to a simmer. When the sugar is dissolved, add the pumpkin and cook gently, stirring and checking frequently, until it is just slightly tender, about 3 minutes. Drain the pumpkin, reserving the liquid. Let cool completely before combining. Store in the refrigerator.

salt-cured chiles

These were introduced to the Lantern kitchen by Fuchsia Dunlop's exhilarating book *Land of Plenty: A Treasury of Authentic Sichuan Cooking.* The surprisingly simple method lets you carry the heat and spice of late summer long into the winter months, such as in Roast Moulard Duck with Kumquats (page 214). Pureed along with cider vinegar, garlic, and a little sugar, salt-cured chiles become a vibrant hot sauce for raw oysters (page 188) or rice and beans.

MAKES 1 QUART

2 pounds fresh red chiles, preferably semi-hot ones such as New Mexico or red cherry, sliced into 1-inch-thick rings
½ cup kosher salt

In a large bowl, combine the chiles and salt, mixing very well with gloved hands or a spoon. Leave out at room temperature for 24 hours and then refrigerate. Mix the chiles once a day for 5 days, or until the salt has dissolved and the now softened chiles are completely covered in liquid. Skim off any white impurities that form at the surface. Transfer to a 1-quart jar with a lid, tamping the chiles down so that they remain 1 inch below the liquid. Keep refrigerated.

chile oil

1 cup expeller-pressed vegetable oil
1 cup extra virgin olive oil
½ cup dried red chile peppers, such as de Arbol, coarsely chopped
1 large mild dried chile, such as Ancho or pasilla
4 garlic cloves, smashed and peeled
1 teaspoon kosher salt

Heat the oils and chiles in a small, heavy pan over medium-low heat until the chiles begin to sizzle. Lower the heat and cook for 5 minutes. Add the garlic and cook for 5 minutes, until it is just light golden. Set aside to cool. Then add the salt and puree with an immersion blender or in a standard blender. Store in the refrigerator.

pickled chile peppers

Both the vinegar and peppers (together or separately) can serve as a condiment for soups like the Red Lentil (page 191), for braised greens and stewed meat, or as a bright winter substitute for dried chiles.

MAKES ABOUT ½ QUART

4 cups loosely packed hot, semi-hot, or sweet fresh chile peppers, with seeds
3 tablespoons kosher salt
¼ cup sugar
4 cups distilled white vinegar

If your chiles are large, cut them into chunks or rounds. If they are small, simply split them in half lengthwise. Put the peppers in one or more jars with tight-fitting lids. In a medium bowl, dissolve the salt and sugar in the vinegar. Pour this over the peppers, close the jar, and refrigerate for at least 1 day before using.

pickled beets

MAKES 2 QUARTS

2 pounds small beets, stems trimmed to ½ inch, peeled, and cut into small wedges
3 tablespoons plus 2 teaspoons kosher salt
1 cup champagne vinegar
¾ cup sugar
1 (2-inch) piece of fresh ginger, cut into ¼-inch-thick coins
6 garlic cloves, smashed and peeled
4 medium dried red chiles, such as de Arbol

Put the beets and the 2 teaspoons salt in a nonreactive 4-quart pot. Add water until the beets are just barely covered and bring to a boil over medium-high heat. Reduce the heat to medium and simmer for 5 to 7 minutes, until the beets are crisp-tender. Drain in a colander, reserving 4½ cups of the cooking liquid. Let the beets cool.

Pour the reserved cooking liquid back into the pot and add the remaining 3 tablespoons salt, the vinegar, and the sugar. Bring to a boil and cook for 30 seconds, stirring until the sugar and salt dissolve. Let cool completely.

Put the beets into a 2-quart jar or other container, layering them with the ginger, garlic, and chiles (smash the chiles if you want spicier beets). Pour in the pickling liquid to cover, screw on the lid, and refrigerate for at least 2 days and up to 1 month.

pickled green tomatoes

MAKES ABOUT 3 QUARTS

4 pounds (about 12) medium green tomatoes, cored
    and cut into 1-inch wedges
4 cups distilled white vinegar
1 cup sugar
4 garlic cloves, smashed and peeled
¾ cup fish sauce
1 tablespoon coriander seeds
2 star anise

Put the tomatoes into a 4-quart stainless-steel or glass container with a tight-fitting lid. In a nonreactive 2-quart pot, combine the vinegar, sugar, garlic, fish sauce, coriander seeds, and star anise. Bring to a boil and cook for 30 seconds, stirring to dissolve the sugar. Pour the hot mixture over the tomatoes. Let cool. Then cover and refrigerate for at least 1 day before serving.

sauerkraut

I love making sauerkraut and wait to do it on a day when I am alone in the kitchen and it's hopefully raining.

MAKES ABOUT 6 QUARTS

2 large heads of cabbage (about 5 pounds), cored and thinly sliced
   (8 quarts loosely packed)
½ cup plus 3 tablespoons kosher salt, or more if needed

Pack the cabbage into a 10- or 12-quart crock or food-safe plastic bucket. Combine the salt with 1 gallon cold water and stir until the salt is completely dissolved. Pour the brine over the cabbage; it should be completely submerged by at least several inches. If not, add more brine, using 2 teaspoons salt for every cup of water. Place a plate on top of the cabbage and push it down so that the cabbage doesn't float to the top. Tuck a large, clean tea towel down around the cabbage using the handle of a long spoon. Add another plate if necessary to keep the towel and any stray cabbage completely submerged. Leave at cool room temperature (68° to 70°F is ideal) in a dark place. Check the cabbage every day or so, removing any mold or impurities that form on the surface. The warmer it is, the faster the sauerkraut will go. After a few days, begin tasting the cabbage; when it reaches a level of tanginess you like, drain the sauerkraut, reserving all the liquid. Pack the kraut into individual containers, about three-quarters full, and cover with the liquid. Store in the refrigerator. For longer storage, bring the liquid to a bare simmer in a large pot over high heat, then lower the heat, and simmer for 2 minutes. Remove from the heat and let cool completely. Fill each container with the cooled brine, submerging the sauerkraut by an inch or so, before refrigerating.

fall

FIRST BITE: SWEET POTATOES PAGE 149
    Whole Roasted Sweet Potatoes with Butter, Molasses,
       and Salt

FALL GREENS PAGE 150
    Braised Chard with Fresh Hot Chiles
    Wilted Baby Collards with Ginger and Shoyu
    Spinach with Melted Leeks and Cardamom

STEAK NIGHT PAGE 155
    Grilled Grass-Fed Porterhouse with Crisp Herbs
    Chocolate and Nuts

JUNK FISH PAGE 159
    Pan-Roasted Black Drum
    Smashed Candy Roaster
    Brussels Sprout Leaves in Brown Butter
    Red Onion Preserves
    Whole Fish Baked in a Salt Crust

GOOD FAT PAGE 166

HEIRLOOM APPLES PAGE 168
    Hard Cider–Braised Pork Shoulder
    Skillet Apples and Onions

COOK A BATCH PAGE 175
    Basic Meat Stock
    Escarole in Broth with Lemon and Eggs
    Basic White Beans with Ham Hocks
    Macaroni with Beans, Roasted Pumpkin, and Ham Hocks
    Old-Fashioned Baked Beans with Smoked Bacon

OYSTERS PAGE 186
    Oyster Stew
    Raw Oysters on Ice with Hot Sauce

CLAY-POT COOKING PAGE 190
    Red Lentil Soup with Smoked Paprika
    Clay-Pot Chicken in Fig Leaves

RED LEAVES PAGE 194
    Red Lettuces with Blue Cheese, Red Grapefruit, and
        Sunflower Sprouts

MEAT AS A CONDIMENT PAGE 196
    White Sweet Potato Soup
    Warm Mushroom Salad with Shallots and Sherry Vinegar
    Pan-Roasted Chicken Livers with Thyme and Schmaltz

SNOW-DAY FOOD PAGE 201
    Pot Roast with Gravy
    Glazed Carrots
    Sour Cream Ice Cream with Sorghum

FIRST BITE:
SWEET POTATOES

Advice books encourage new parents to feed their babies limp allergen-free processed rice cereal for their first bite of solid food. When Oona was ready, we dutifully bought a box, but at the last minute, we roasted her a sweet potato instead. Before boxed flakes, sweet potatoes must have been the classic first food. They are earthy, fruity, and gently sweet like milk, but with a novel new texture. Guaranteed photo op.

I've never met a sweet potato that I didn't like, but the Carolina Ruby and the creamy white-fleshed Hayman are all-stars. Straight from the ground, freshly dug sweet potatoes are dry, starchy, and not sweet at all. They get their flavor and richness during a several-week curing process, ideally in a humid cellar first, then in a dry basement or outdoor lean-to. As they ripen, they lose starch and grow sweeter every day. One farmer I know stores them under his old wide wooden front porch, where they keep perfectly into March—and then on my counter for weeks longer. One of the most nutritious things you can eat, they are a "perfect food" that goes sweet, savory, or, as in the recipe below, both ways.

whole roasted sweet potatoes
with butter, molasses, and salt

If I have the oven on anyway, I will throw a couple sweet potatoes in and let them bake at whatever temperature until they are done. To cook the sweet potatoes on their own, prick them a few times, lightly oil their skins, and place them directly on the top rack in a hot oven (400°F) with a pan placed below them on the next rack to catch any drips. Bake for 40 to 50 minutes, or until they are completely tender, slightly shrunken, with crisp skin. (For a quick—and more energy-efficient—meal for one, microwave a medium sweet potato on high power for 5 minutes; then turn it over and cook for another 4 to 5 minutes. Let it sit for a few minutes to collect itself.) Split the top, insert some butter, drizzle with a little molasses or sorghum, and add a generous sprinkle of kosher or sea salt. Save any surplus roasted potatoes for a mashed sweet potato side dish, to thicken a spicy shrimp chowder, or to add heft to a batch of buttermilk biscuits.

FALL GREENS

In the South, we don't get many greens during the hot summer, so early fall means leafy relief from the dense, ever-bigger eggplants and squashes. I cooked my first greens of the season today at the SEEDS (South Eastern Efforts Developing Sustainable Spaces) garden in downtown Durham. It's an oasis of fig trees, sunflowers, rows of lettuces, tomatoes, okra, summer and winter squash, yard-long beans, and black-eyed peas in the middle of a food desert. Because this part of town is a bus ride from the closest grocery store, some neighbors get many of their meals from gas stations and convenience stores.

Here in the garden, thirty teenagers meet each day after school to tend to their crops and rotate shifts getting up at 5 a.m. on Saturdays to sell their vegetables at the Durham farmers' market. They grow twelve different kinds of hot and sweet peppers—including sweet Marconi and spicy Jamaican Hot Chocolate—such a bountiful crop that it helps their bottom line to find ways of preserving them. Today, we worked on some ideas for their imminent harvest: pickled and salt-cured chile peppers (pages 140, 141) and, since it was lunchtime, an all-garden meal of red chard braised with fresh hot peppers and garlic. We simmered the greens until they were sweet, tender, dark forest green.

Although a few kids had never tasted the chard they grow, most had. When someone doesn't like a new flavor, Kavanah Ramsier, the group's leader, asks them to explain why. This usually requires another taste, after which the taster often just gives up and likes it. But as long as they try it and think about it, not lik-ing a vegetable is no big deal—there is a lot to choose from in the garden. School gardeners are a nonchalant breed, and Kavanah's cool reminded me of the tortured dinner Oona and I had a few days ago when I watched her pick fifty gnat-size pieces of carrot out of her chicken soup. Fully aware of her burgeoning plain-food fetish, I had gone ahead and added the spoonful of minced car-rot anyway, proving that I am more compulsive than she is. Kavanah wisely takes the long view, having learned that if you go to the mat with kids about food, you have already lost. She lowers the stakes, knowing that one day she will neutrally reintroduce the offender, maybe waiting until late fall to give a kid a face-saver; after all, greens are sweeter after the first frost.

braised chard with fresh hot chiles

SERVES 4 AS A SIDE DISH

2 tablespoons olive oil
4 garlic cloves, thinly sliced
1 semi-hot fresh red chile, such as Fresno, or more to taste, sliced into thick rounds
2 big bunches of chard (about 25 stems total), stemmed, leaves torn into big pieces
    and stems thinly sliced
1 medium tomato, diced
Kosher salt and freshly ground black pepper

Heat a large sauté pan over medium heat, and add the oil and then the garlic and chile.
Stirring frequently, cook until the chile has softened and the garlic is golden, 1 to 2 minutes.
Add the chard stems, the tomato, and then the chard leaves. Season to taste with salt and
pepper, and toss to coat with the oil. Reduce the heat to medium-low and simmer, tossing
frequently with tongs, for 3 to 4 minutes, until the chard is tender. Using tongs, transfer the
chard to a warm shallow bowl, letting the juice and most of the tomatoes and peppers fall
back into the pan. Reduce the liquid in the pan over high heat for 2 minutes, or until it is
slightly syrupy (about ⅓ cup). Pour the sauce over the chard, and serve.

wilted baby collards
with ginger and shoyu

The ideal size for the collards here is nine inches long. If substituting larger leaves, blanch them a bit longer and continue to sauté them until tender, adding a little water or stock if necessary.

SERVES 4 AS A SIDE DISH

2 pounds baby collard greens, stemmed, leaves cut into ½-inch-wide strips
2 tablespoons plus 2 teaspoons shoyu soy sauce, or less if substituting
    regular soy sauce
½ teaspoon toasted sesame oil
2 tablespoons expeller-pressed vegetable oil
2 scant tablespoons very thinly julienned fresh ginger
2 dried red chiles, such as de Arbol, crumbled into small pieces
Kosher salt
⅔ cup chicken stock, preferably homemade (page 177)

Blanch the collards for 30 seconds in a large pot of salted boiling water. Drain, and then quickly transfer them to an ice bath. As soon as they are cold, drain again and gently squeeze them with your hands to remove as much moisture as possible. Transfer the collards to a medium bowl and toss with your fingers to separate, adding the shoyu and sesame oil and thoroughly distributing them.

Heat the vegetable oil in a medium sauté pan over medium-low heat. Add the ginger and chiles. Sauté for a minute, until the ginger is wilted and fragrant but has not colored. Raise the heat to medium and add the collards. Season with salt and toss to coat and incorporate the ginger and chiles. Add the chicken stock and cook, stirring frequently, for about 3 minutes, until the greens are very hot. Season with additional salt if necessary.

spinach with melted leeks and cardamom

Dark green curly spinach varieties like Savoy or Bloomsdale have a deeper, richer flavor than the lighter green, grassier flat-leaf spinach, but any spinach pairs wonderfully with cardamom.

SERVES 4 AS A SIDE DISH

2 tablespoons unsalted butter
1 medium leek, cut into thin rounds, well washed, and drained
Kosher salt
1 pound spinach, trimmed, washed, and drained
Freshly ground black pepper
½ cup crème fraîche, store-bought or homemade (page 224)
¾ teaspoon ground cardamom, or more to taste

Melt 1 tablespoon of the butter in a large sauté pan or skillet with a lid over low heat. Add the leeks and season with ¼ teaspoon salt. Cover tightly and gently sweat, stirring the leeks occasionally, until they are very soft, about 15 minutes. If the leeks begin to color at all, lower the heat and add a tablespoon of water. Transfer to a plate and wipe out the pan.

Raise the heat to medium-high and swirl the remaining 1 tablespoon butter in the pan. Add the spinach, starting with as much as will easily fit. Season it with ¼ teaspoon salt and a little fresh pepper and toss, adding the remaining spinach as the first batch wilts. Add ¼ teaspoon salt and more pepper, and as soon as all the spinach is completely wilted, remove from the stove and pour off any accumulated liquid.

Reduce the heat to low and return the leeks to the pan. Stir in the crème fraîche and cardamom. Adjust the seasoning and cook for 1 minute, until very hot.

STEAK NIGHT

Tonight we have a big gang of meat-eaters at the table and I plan on enjoying every minute. I love cooking steak for dinner parties—it's a splurge but also fast and straightforward to prepare. Instead of buying six or eight skinny steaks that are easy to overcook and that some guests won't finish, grilling one very thick bone-in porterhouse provides satisfyingly hefty slices of evenly rosy, well-charred but juicy meat. Reasonable portions and less waste also allow room in the budget for better-quality meat. Using dry-aged grass-fed beef for this meal might cost about $50 but will feed as many as eight people when paired with big, tender white beans (see page 180) and some lightly dressed fresh arugula or spinach. After dinner we will have fresh black and purple muscadines and bronze scuppernong grapes from John Ferguson with big chunks of chocolate and roasted filberts.

grilled grass-fed porterhouse with crisp herbs

SERVES 6 TO 8

1 (2- to 2½-pound) grass-fed porterhouse or T-bone steak, 2 to 3 inches thick
Kosher salt and freshly ground black pepper
½ cup extra virgin olive oil
Leaves from 1 bunch of fresh sage (about 1½ cups)
Leaves from 1 bunch of fresh rosemary (about 1½ cups)
Flaky sea salt, such as Maldon, for serving

At least an hour and up to several hours before dinner, place the steak on a platter and cover it with a generous amount of salt and pepper and a little of the olive oil, keeping in mind that a thick steak can take a shocking amount of seasoning.

Prepare a hot fire in a charcoal grill, arranging most of the coals on one half and just a few on the other side.

When the grill is very hot, but the flame has died down and the coals are completely covered with ash, put the steak on the hot side of the grill with the smaller tenderloin side on the cooler part. Watch closely for flare-ups, extinguishing them with a squirt bottle or teacup of water or by briefly covering the grill with its lid. Cook the steak for about 6 minutes, giving it a quarter turn once but still keeping the skinny fillet side away from the hottest part of the grill. Flip the steak, keeping it on the hot part of the grill, until it is just seared, 3 to 4 minutes. Move it to the cool side of the grill to finish cooking to the desired doneness (about 5 minutes, or 125°F on an instant-read thermometer, for medium-rare).

Transfer the steak to a carving board set in a warm spot in the kitchen, tent it loosely with aluminum foil or parchment, and allow it to rest for 10 to 15 minutes (during which time the internal temperature will continue to rise). When the steak is done resting, slice it against the grain, leaving it arranged around the bone.

While you are slicing, slowly heat the remaining olive oil in a small sauté pan over low heat. When the oil is hot but not smoking, raise the heat slightly and add the sage leaves and swirl them in the pan, covering them with the oil. Reduce the heat. As soon as they start to go from light gray-green to a deeper bright green, use a slotted spoon to transfer them to a paper towel to drain. Repeat the process with the rosemary leaves. Pour the hot oil over the sliced steak, and top with the crisp herbs and a sprinkling of salt.

chocolate and nuts

I try to always keep a few thick pieces of chocolate—dark and milk—in the kitchen for an easy, satisfying snack or dessert. A hefty piece of chocolate breaks apart into chunky shards and pairs nicely with roasted nuts and a bit of seasonal fruit: blackberries or cherries in summer, tangerines or preserved pears in winter, and in North Carolina in fall, the gorgeous family of native grapes known as muscadines.

JUNK FISH

Mac and I got married ten years ago tonight in a small, old fishing town just south of the Outer Banks of North Carolina. Beaufort stayed pretty quiet from the end of the Civil War, when it was occupied by Union forces, until a few years before we got married, when the remains of Blackbeard's ship were discovered two miles offshore. We had our rehearsal dinner in nearby Morehead City at the Sanitary Fish Market, where our guests—many tipsy Yankees who had misjudged the power of bourbon and ginger ale— had to choose among croaker, black drum, jumping mullet, and a bony but yummy number known locally as "spots." There were a lot of off-the-menu requests for tuna. Back then, strange sea creatures that hit the dinner table were often still called "junk fish," but you don't hear the term as often anymore as "new" fish rocket from obscurity to cultish to overfished popularity in just a few years. In North Carolina in the 1970s bluefin tuna—one of the original "junk" starlets—was pursued mainly by sportsmen who had to pay to have their catch hauled away after the photo was taken. Now well on our way to enjoying tuna and many other former junk fish into commercial extinction, the term is nearly anachronistic.

It is clear that finding a way to enjoy a wider variety of seafood (while not gorging on any one in particular) will be one key to the long-term health of the oceans. In *Chez Panisse Cooking*, chef and salumi-maker Paul Bertolli offers a loving description of the perfect fish soup that is also great advice for how to best eat from the sea: "Fish soup mirrors the ocean . . . just as there are kelp beds and reefs populated by a diversity of colorful rockfish and crustaceans and quieter, clearer tide pools, so there are soups that vary in their complexity and flavor and variety of elements."

Some of the delicious things that find their way into my kitchen are speckled sea trout, eel, squid, and razor-back butterfish in the winter, and then in the summer star butterfish, sheepshead, croaker, porgy, red mullet, and bluefish when they are running. Tonight we have black drum from Pamlico Sound, just north of Beaufort. Black drum is a savory, versatile fish: it will hold up on the grill and pairs well with ripe cherry tomatoes marinated with chopped hot green chiles; in colder weather I like to roast it whole, packed in salt. Salt crusts don't make a fish salty as you might assume, but insulate it from the heat of the oven, allowing it to cook gently in its own juices; you will never eat a moister fish.

pan-roasted black drum

Black drum is a terrific fish—meaty and satisfying but still delicate. It's often compared to overfished grouper but is more flavorful and less tough, and its skin cooks up crisp and savory. If you can't find drum, black cod (sablefish) from Alaska or wild striped bass is a good substitute.

SERVES 2

1 pound black drum fillet, skin on
Kosher salt and freshly ground black pepper
1 tablespoon expeller-pressed vegetable oil
3 fresh bay leaves, or another hearty herb like winter savory or a few sturdy sprigs of thyme
1 tablespoon unsalted butter

Preheat the oven to 450°F.

Rinse the fish and pat it dry. Leave the fillet whole and score it lengthwise on the skin side with a shallow 3- to 4-inch-long slit to minimize curling. Season it generously on both sides with salt and pepper. Heat a large cast-iron skillet over medium-high heat and add the oil, coating the pan. Lay the fish in the pan, skin side down, and cook it for about 3 minutes or until it is golden brown and releases easily with a spatula. Flip the fish, and tuck 2 of the bay leaves underneath and place the other one on top. Dot the top of the fillet with the butter, and after it melts, tilt the pan and use a spoon to baste the fish a few times with the fat and juices. Transfer the pan to the oven and roast for about 4 minutes, until the fish is just done and the tip of a sharp knife left in the middle of the thickest part for a few seconds comes out warm to the touch. Transfer the fish to a warm platter, removing and discarding the bay leaves.

smashed candy roaster

Candy roaster pie has been an Appalachian Thanksgiving tradition for a hundred years. The term describes several varieties of large super-sweet winter squash. Many are so big—thirty pounds or more—that some farmers sell them at the market already cut into wedges. Any dense eating pumpkin or winter squash works well here.

SERVES 2 GENEROUSLY, WITH LOTS OF LEFTOVERS

3 pounds seeded candy roaster or other dense, sweet pumpkin or winter squash,
    cut into large wedges
Extra virgin olive oil
Kosher salt and freshly ground black pepper
Crème fraîche, store-bought or homemade (page 224)

Preheat the oven to 375°F.

Put the candy roaster wedges on a baking sheet, drizzle generously with olive oil, and season with salt and pepper. Roast until very soft and caramelized, 1 hour or longer. Let the squash cool, and then scoop the flesh into a sieve or strainer, avoiding any crispy or dry pieces from the end. Allow it to sit there for 10 minutes to drain.

Put the drained squash in a bowl and mash with a potato masher or a stiff whisk. Season with salt and pepper, and finish with crème fraîche (1 tablespoon or so for every 2 cups mashed candy roaster).

brussels sprout leaves in brown butter

Browning butter is one of the fastest, simplest ways of creating deep, satisfying flavor. Removing the leaves from Brussels sprouts allows them to cook quickly and evenly, avoiding the overcooking and resulting mushiness that many associate with the vegetable.

SERVES 2

1 pound Brussels sprouts
3 tablespoons unsalted butter
Kosher salt

With a sharp paring knife, trim the Brussels sprouts and cut out a deep V-shaped notch in the bottom of each one. Peel the leaves from each one, leaving the small core whole if it doesn't easily separate.

Heat a large skillet over medium-low heat and add the butter, swirling it while it slowly cooks and becomes fragrant and light brown, about 2 minutes. Add the leaves, season with salt, and toss to combine. Raise the heat to medium-high, cover the pan, and don't move it until the leaves wilt, 1 to 2 minutes. If none of the leaves have browned yet, uncover the pan, raise the heat to high, and cook, tossing, until the leaves are crisp-tender, have turned bright green, and many are lightly caramelized. Season again if necessary before serving.

red onion preserves

These preserves will keep for a few weeks in the refrigerator and are good on a grilled cheese sandwich or as a condiment for creamy pureed white beans.

MAKES 3 TO 4 CUPS

2 tablespoons extra virgin olive oil
4 medium red onions, thinly sliced
1 garlic clove
1 dried red chile pepper, such as de Arbol
Kosher salt
1 cup dry red wine
¼ cup red wine vinegar
¼ cup honey
2 teaspoons coriander seeds, lightly toasted and ground

Heat a medium-size heavy pot over low heat and add the oil, onions, garlic, and chile; season with salt. Cover and cook gently until the onions are very soft and tender, about 5 minutes. Add the wine, vinegar, honey, and coriander. Raise the heat slightly and cook, uncovered, until the liquid is syrupy, about 15 minutes. Store refrigerated for up to a week.

whole fish baked in a salt crust

Rip the top off a whole box of kosher salt and dump it into a big bowl. Add 2 large beaten egg whites and combine, using your hands or the hands of nearby children, until the salt has the texture of wet sand. Oil your scaled and gutted fish (a 3-pounder will be generous for two but can work for a lighter meal for four) and tuck herbs and/or sliced citrus into the cavity. Line a sturdy rimmed baking sheet with parchment and arrange a fish-shaped layer of salt on it. Place the fish on top and then mound the rest of the salt on top and gently pack it down so that the fish is completely enclosed. Bake it in a preheated 400°F oven for 7 to 8 minutes per pound, until the fish smells delicious and the salt crust is hard and golden brown.

At the table, crack the crust with the back of a big serving spoon and remove the pieces of salt. Gently lift serving-size hunks of fish directly onto warm plates, and serve along with some good olive oil or garlic mayonnaise and, yes, a bit more salt.

GOOD FAT

I drive out to the edge of town to pick up our weekly gallon of grass-fed milk from our dairy co-op. It's extremely rich and extremely fatty—in other words, extremely delicious. But the fat on its own is not something I worry about. Yes, there is an enormous health crisis in our country today, and it's fueled in large part by a diet that is increasingly full of processed food. But young children need natural fats from real, unprocessed food for proper growth and development, and we all require them for healthy brain and immune-system function, hormone regulation, digestion, and healing. Fats play an essential role in unlocking the nutrients in many vegetables. Those of us who prefer to eat our vegetables warm from the pot with a drizzle of walnut oil or pat of butter get more out of them than the spartans who dutifully crunch their green beans and cauliflower raw and undressed.

I can't imagine life without fat—the crunchy skin of a fresh roasted ham, steamed whole milk in strong coffee, a BLT with mayo, cold heavy cream on blueberries, or the combination of a juicy grilled steak and its melting, crisp edge. But not all animal fat is created equal. Eggs from chickens raised outdoors on pasture and forage have many times more nutrients and flavor than their industrially raised counterparts. Milk and meat from cows that graze on green pasture are higher in omega-3s, or "good fats," than that from cows fed soy and corn. The kinds of fat you choose are more important than the amount: meals made from real foods that include wholesome fats are more delicious, but also more healthy, than a diet misted with spray vegetable oil.

Now, in nearly the same time it took to read my fat rant, you could have made some butter.

This week, I begged for a half-gallon of yellow cream in addition to our milk. It's grassy and thick, perfect for butter. To develop the flavor, I left it out on the counter overnight. Since it was raw and still alive, eventually it would have soured on its own, but I helped it along with a little buttermilk.

By morning, the cream had thickened and gained a cultured tang. For even more flavor, I could have left it in a cool spot all weekend, but we were in a hurry. I set the bowl of cream over some ice to chill a bit, then set up a food processor and a stand mixer for a butter race between Oona and her friend Gabe. After they washed their hands, we divided the cream into the bowls of the two machines—one quart in each, the most that you could manage in one batch—and let the challenge begin. During butter making, cream quickly morphs through a few stages: sloshy, then softly whipped, and then at the two-minute mark, overwhipped and chunky. By the time the stopwatch read four minutes precisely, the whipped cream had suddenly separated into butter and buttermilk in both machines. We drained the different butters into separate colanders, saving the tart buttermilk, with its yellow flecks of butter, in a big pitcher. (Commercial buttermilk has never seen butter but is made by culturing skim milk, sometimes also thickened with stabilizers.) The kids then each kneaded their own ball of butter in ice water to rinse it of the remaining buttermilk (which would render it less creamy and shorten its shelf life). When tasting the butters side by side on cornbread, Oona and Gabe expressed a strong preference for whichever one was in their mouths at the time. Still hungry, we made pancakes with the buttermilk.

The cream cost $14 and made about two pounds of butter, double the price of store-bought, but it has at least twice the flavor and probably nutrition too, and came with a bonus quart of buttermilk good enough to drink in a glass, icy and straight. Homemade butter keeps for about a week, and you will serve it with everything: in fall, on a sandwich with thinly sliced ham; in winter, melted on a bowl of hot popcorn; in spring, with spicy radishes and salt; and in the summertime, spread on ears of steamed corn.

HEIRLOOM APPLES

These days, Arthur refuses to eat anything cut into baby-size pieces, demanding that all food be served "wholebig" and thus fully choke-able. Today, on a visit to Diane Flynt's Foggy Ridge Cider, he was in heaven, crawling on the ground in the orchard and eating the fallen fruit. He would take just one bite of each before throwing it down and picking up another. At Foggy Ridge—which is just a few miles off the Blue Ridge Parkway— Diane makes delicate small-batch hard apple ciders that drink like Champagne. When Arthur finally found an apple that he liked enough to continue to eat, it wasn't surprising that it was one that had already begun to ferment. Alcohol aside, he had never tasted anything like Diane's apples. She grows old English varieties like Roxbury Russets and Cox's Orange Pippin. In Lee Calhoun's opinion, she has the best-looking orchard he's ever seen.

That really means something. Lee—who lives just south of Chapel Hill in Pittsboro— authored the instant classic *Old Southern Apples,* and he and his wife, Edith, have created a huge database of old apple varieties in order to cross-reference and catalog new discoveries. It was from him that I learned that by the end of the late nineteenth century, more than 1,800 different kinds of apples were growing here in the South, most of them bred and so named here: Maiden's Blush, Hewe's Crab, Green Cheese, Hollow Log, Alexander's Ice Cream, July/August-Go-No-Further, and, my favorite, the golf ball–size sweet-tart Golden Harvey. Today only about 200 of those varieties remain, many saved from extinction by Lee. Married for more than fifty years, Edith and Lee have their own orchard of 250 heirloom southern apples plus peaches, pears, damsons, figs, grapes, cherries, blueberries, even Japanese persimmons. An energetic seventy-five, Lee just finished building a few hundred-foot rows of raised beds in his backyard so that he can continue gardening in his old age.

Lee usually hears about a new old tree by word of mouth—a friend of a friend remembers hearing their grandfather describe the best apple he ever ate just north of West Jefferson or behind the old Chatham County courthouse. When he finds the tree, it is often a hundred years old, down a dirt road, and quite possibly dying—one time, next to a front porch where a man sat skinning a muskrat; another time, sharing a pasture with two gigantic hogs a farmer was fattening with piles of stale doughnuts from a nearby bakery. Lee is currently revising his book; since he included his home phone number in the introduction to the first edition, his apple roster has increased exponentially.

Why did almost 2,000 different apples once thrive in the South? Lee explains that for a few hundred years, these apples were essential to survival. In 1750 most everyone lived on a farm and grew apples—a typical farm grew about 40 different varieties. As the seasons progressed, the apples ripened, providing a bit of fresh fruit year-round: from apples for eating off the tree in early June to the hardy "keepers" that ripened in late October and could last into deep winter. Products made from apples provided food all year long: cider vinegar, which preserved food for the winter; kegs of fortifying cider, both sweet and hard; cloth bags of dried apples; and crocks of applesauce and apple butter to sweeten the dull flavors of winter's preserved foods.

Before nurseries (and the practice of grafting) were established in the South in the mid-nineteenth century, the only way to grow a new apple tree was to plant a seed and then wait five or six years to discover what kind of apple you were growing; while the apple that contributed the seed you had planted was your new tree's mother, the father could be any nearby tree. So for roughly three hundred years in the South, an enormous apple breeding experiment took place as settlers fanned out and planted valuable, portable apple seeds: literally millions of unique apple trees were the result. Most were terrible, but many were brilliant and those were saved and nurtured. When grafting became widespread, apple growers could finally choose which varieties to plant. These survivors are called heirlooms because that's literally what they were. A pot containing a cutting from a family's favorite tree—very often they were the only ones who grew it—was a common wedding gift to a daughter or son before they left home.

The term *heirloom* can feel a little bit dusty, but spending some time with people like Lee and Diane will convince you that protecting these hardy varieties is all about the future. Two thirds of the world's apples are now grown in China, which also produces about half of the juice we drink in the U.S. Relying on a dwindling number of varieties of any important food crop has been a disaster in the past, but seems especially risky now, when we need biodiversity more than ever in order to adapt to our rapidly changing climate and world.

Lee Calhoun became an apple hunter because he couldn't find any old varieties at nurseries. There is no such thing as an apple seed bank: the only way to preserve an apple is on a living tree. Lee helped create the Southern Heritage Apple Orchard, where the eight hundred trees he donated and grafted now grow and to which he adds a few new ones every year. You might think that an heirloom apple hunter would be precious about the idea of traditional varieties, but Lee is not; in his own garden alongside his antique crops he plants modern vegetable varieties like Celebrity tomatoes and Bodacious sweet corn. Lee grows his old apple trees for practical purposes: they are the ones that will thrive in his backyard.

hard cider–braised pork shoulder

Pork shoulder is my hands-down favorite cut of meat. Studded with garlic, it makes a succulent roast for dinner with enough for sandwiches the next day; and braised with a few flavorful ingredients, it creates its own sauce. Hard cider brings acidity to the sweetness of regular cider and apples.

SERVES 8

1 (5- to 6-pound) boneless pork shoulder
3 garlic cloves, each cut lengthwise into 3 or 4 slivers, plus 1 head of garlic, unpeeled,
    cut in half crosswise
Kosher salt and freshly ground black pepper
2 tablespoons expeller-pressed vegetable oil
1 yellow onion, quartered
1 carrot, thickly sliced
1 tart apple, cut into big chunks
1 cup apple cider, preferably unpasteurized
2 cups hard apple cider

Rinse the pork and pat it dry. Using a thin, sharp boning knife, make ten to twelve deep, narrow slits in the pork and insert a sliver of garlic into each. Season the meat generously all over with salt and pepper, and then use kitchen twine to tie the shoulder into a compact, uniform shape. If it isn't already, allow it to come to room temperature.

Heat a large, heavy Dutch oven over medium-high heat. Add the oil and sear the pork on all sides, taking your time, turning it frequently and adjusting the heat as necessary to avoid scorching. Done properly, this will take about 20 minutes.

Meanwhile, preheat the oven to 300°F.

Transfer the pork to a large plate. Pour off all but 1 tablespoon of the fat in the pan, and add the onion, carrot, and apple. Season with salt and pepper, and sauté over medium heat until they are golden brown and soft, 3 to 4 minutes. Add both ciders and the halved head of garlic, and bring to a simmer. Return the pork to the pan. Put a piece of parchment or aluminum foil over the meat, folding it down around it so that it makes a snug tent. Cover the pot with a tight-fitting lid, and place it in the middle of the oven. Cook until the pork is very tender, about 3 hours, turning it once or twice to keep all sides moist.

Transfer the meat to a platter to rest before slicing. Strain the broth, discarding the apple and vegetables. Skim the fat from the pan juices and return the juices to the pan. Over medium heat, reduce to about 2 cups. Adjust the seasoning, and serve with the pork.

skillet apples and onions

SERVES 8 AS A SIDE DISH

5 to 6 tart, firm apples, like Arkansas Black or Granny Smith
3 tablespoons lard or bacon fat
3 yellow onions, sliced into ¼-inch rings
Kosher salt
Light brown sugar, optional

Using an apple corer, core the apples. Slice them into 1-inch-thick rings. (Do not peel.)

Heat a large cast-iron skillet over medium-high heat, add ½ tablespoon of the lard and half of the onions, season with salt, and sauté until fragrant and starting to lightly color, about 3 minutes. Push the onions to one side of the pan, raise the heat to high, and add 1 tablespoon of the lard and half of the apples, tossing to coat them with the fat and seasoning with salt and a little brown sugar if desired. Cook until the apples are just tender, 5 to 7 minutes, turning as necessary. Keep the apples and onions warm on a platter or in a low oven while repeating with the remaining ingredients.

COOK A BATCH

Before I had kids, I didn't get the idea of "saving time in the kitchen"—sorry, say that again? I spent as much time there as I could and we ate dinner at nine or ten o'clock. We were happy like that for years, until we had Oona and Arthur and then suddenly there were lots of hungry, tired people around who were ready for dinner in what felt like the middle of the day. We had just opened the restaurant, and so on the rare nights I was at home, we ate takeout or eggs and toast. Dinner went from being the whole point of my day to something to check off the list.

When I found a little more time, I began experimenting with cooking batches of food that would give us a head start on those hungry late afternoons. Now, every couple of days, I make a big pot of something that can easily become a quick meal with a few last-minute additions. Last Saturday was the first cold day of fall, and I cooked a batch of brothy black beans, made rich with smoked ham hocks. The combination is so tasty to me that I have eaten it every day for lunch since, alternating between cilantro and hot sauce and grated cheddar cheese and salted red onion as condiments. I fed the beans to Arthur straight up—perfect "finger food"—and also to Oona as a filling for soft corn tortillas. Then today in the midst of a crazy mini heat wave (88°F!), I pureed them with some broth, sherry, and a splash of cream to make a last-minute cold soup for friends before dinner.

Making a pot of beans, a deeply flavored stock, or a big bowl of fluffy rice is a simple task that is the best kind of easy project: absorbing in its simplicity but that can still be accomplished during a phone call or while unloading the dishwasher. Small chunks of pork shoulder, salted overnight, can be cooked under fat for a few hours in a slow oven and then stored under the same fat for several weeks in the fridge. With almost no effort, the preserved pork can be heated in its fat and spread on toast, added to sautéed sauerkraut (see page 143) with sausage and baked, or sautéed until crispy and served with boiled baby potatoes or stewed with flageolet beans. But while meats and vegetables can work well, stocks, beans, peas, lentils, grains, and bones are the all-stars of big-batch cooking; they keep for a week in the fridge and offer many possibilities.

MAKING STOCK

A smoky turkey cooked on our Weber grill last Thanksgiving made a broth so good that I froze it in small containers and parceled it out for months: in a meaty but otherwise meat-less stew with hominy and squash, as a hot mug of plain broth with sea salt for the hungry cook, or in egg noodles glazed with butter and tossed with tender herbs. I remember that this particular bird—a Bourbon Red, raised outdoors—had cost a gasping $140 (I had to leave the market to hit the cash machine before I could take it home). But I ended up with a holiday meal for twenty, days of my mom's hot turkey and gravy on toast for houseguests, and then many more stock-based meals, making its cost more like a down payment than a splurge.

Unlike most vegetable broths or bouillon cubes, homemade broth is a delicious and energizing food. If you are starting with raw bones instead of a leftover carcass, try to buy the bones from a nearby small-scale producer: your stock will have more flavor and nutrition, and the farm gains income from a part of the animal they need to sell to make raising the rest (chops, steaks, chicken breasts) economically viable. In fact, the best and most nutritious meat stock can include the very things that are hardest for farmers to sell: fresh chicken and pork feet, beef shanks, and ham bones.

basic meat stock

For the bones, select a combination of the following: chicken (necks, whole carcasses, wings, or feet), pork (any bone, shanks, necks, split feet, smoked hock, or ham bone), or beef (oxtail or any bones).

MAKES 6 QUARTS

5 pounds meaty bones
1 carrot
1 onion, halved
1 celery stalk or leek, trimmed
1 head of garlic, unpeeled, sliced in half crosswise
2 dried bay leaves or a few slices of fresh ginger, optional
5 black peppercorns
Kosher salt

Put the bones in a stockpot, add about 6 quarts cold water to cover by an inch, and place over high heat. Bring to a bare simmer and then reduce the heat to low, so that the water is just gently bubbling. Simmer for 5 minutes and then skim it for the next 10 to 15 minutes or until perfectly clear. Add the remaining ingredients, season with a little salt, and cook for 2 hours or longer, until very flavorful. Cool, strain, and season again before refrigerating for up to several days or freezing for up to 2 months.

VARIATIONS
Turkey Stock: Substitute a cooked turkey carcass for the bones.

Dark Poultry Stock or Dark Pork Stock: Roast poultry or pork bones (or a combination) on a baking sheet in a 450°F oven for 30 to 45 minutes until they are a uniform deep golden brown. Deglaze the sheet pan with water, and place the bones and liquid in a stockpot. Add water to cover by an inch, and follow the basic recipe.

escarole in broth
with lemon and eggs

SERVES 4 AS AN APPETIZER OR 2 AS AN ENTRÉE

4 large eggs
4 cups rich chicken or meat stock, preferably homemade (page 177)
2 garlic cloves, smashed and peeled
½ lemon
1 head of escarole, washed and torn into bite-size pieces
Kosher salt and freshly ground black pepper
Grated aged sheep's-milk cheese, such as the pecorino from Dancing Ewe Farm,
    for serving

Beat the eggs with ½ cup of the stock in a bowl.

In a heavy 4-quart pot, bring the remaining 3½ cups stock and the garlic to a simmer over medium-high heat. Using a sharp vegetable peeler, remove the zest from the lemon in big strips, taking care to avoid the white pith. Add the zest to the stock and simmer over low heat for 3 to 4 minutes. While it cooks, juice the lemon half and set the juice aside.

Add the escarole to the simmering stock and season with salt and pepper. Cook the escarole for 2 to 3 minutes, until it is wilted and tender. Remove from the heat and add half of the egg mixture in a slow, thin stream around the pot, waiting 5 seconds or so before giving it a gentle stir with a spoon in one direction. Repeat with the remaining egg mixture, cooking until the broth has thickened slightly and is full of silky strands of egg. Gently stir in the lemon juice, check the seasoning, and remove the garlic and lemon zest. Divide among warm bowls and serve topped with the cheese.

NOTES ON BEANS AND GRAINS

Since this cooking is so elemental, the quality of the ingredients is especially important. Beans and grains can hibernate in the distribution pipeline for years, so try to buy from a store that has high turnover or from mail-order sources that grow their own. Heirloom beans from growers like Rancho Gordo in California and old-fashioned grains from Anson Mills in South Carolina are a breed apart.

At Anson Mills, Glenn Roberts mills a whole galaxy of insanely flavorful grains, including Carolina Gold rice, which was regarded as the finest rice in the world until the Civil War. Simply boiled and served with a little butter and salt, the rice—known in South Carolina as "Charleston ice cream"—is an incredible meal all by itself. Working with about thirty organic growers in six states, Glenn also cultivates brawny whole hominy grits and other vanishing varieties of corn, rice, and wheat, Japanese buckwheat, French oatmeal, and Italian farro. He is also bringing back tiny Sea Island red peas—the rich, nutty relation of today's bland yet stinky commercial black-eyed pea and the original pea used for hoppin' John. While field peas thrive here in the Carolinas, our sticky clay soils and pests make growing regular shell beans, like navy, pinto, and black beans, a challenge, but there are many small-scale artisan producers cropping up in bean-growing parts of the country. I mail-order ours from Rancho Gordo, where they grow and sell fast-cooking "fresh" dried beans in varieties like the rosy, juicy Lila and the meaty Scarlet Runner.

basic white beans with ham hocks

Canned beans can't compete with dried ones on flavor, versatility, or price. Cooking times for dried beans vary greatly depending on the variety and on how long they have been stored: the fresher they are, the faster they cook. This recipe can be used with any white-ish or cranberry-type bean, and the general method can be used for any dried beans with variations on the seasonings: pair pink varieties like pintos or kidneys with smoked bacon, oregano, and beer; season pale green flageolets with stewed leeks and fennel. *Heirloom Beans*, by Steve Sando of Rancho Gordo, is a good resource for bean cookery.

MAKES 4 QUARTS, WITH LIQUID

2 pounds dried white beans or large limas
2 very large, meaty smoked ham hocks (about 2 pounds total)
1 small carrot
1 medium yellow onion
1 small head of garlic, unpeeled, cut in half crosswise
1 small celery stalk
2 dried bay leaves
10 black peppercorns
1 dried red chile, such as de árbol
Zest of ½ lemon, removed in strips with a vegetable peeler
1 cup dry white wine
Kosher salt

Pick through the beans and remove any debris. If you have time to soak the beans overnight, place them in a large pot, add cold water to cover generously, and let sit for 12 hours or overnight. Otherwise, to quick-soak the beans, put them in a heavy 6-quart pot and add water to cover by about 2 inches. Bring to a boil and then turn the heat off. Let soak for 1 hour and then drain in a colander.

Whichever method you used, drain the beans, return them to the pot, and cover with water by about 1 inch. Bring to a simmer over medium heat and cook for several minutes, skimming off any foam that rises to the top. Add the ham hocks if you are using them, along with the carrot, onion, garlic, celery, bay leaves, peppercorns, and chile. Simmer for 30 minutes to 1 hour or longer, until the beans are nearly tender, adding a little water as necessary along the way so that the beans remain submerged. When the beans are tender but still just slightly too firm to eat, add the lemon zest, white wine, and 2 tablespoons salt and continue to simmer until they are completely cooked. Adjust the seasoning and remove the carrot, onion, garlic, celery, bay leaves, chile, and as many of the peppercorns as you easily find.

If you find that the beans are done before the ham hocks are completely tender, transfer the hocks to a small saucepan along with some bean cooking liquid and additional water to cover. Simmer gently until the meat is fork-tender; let the hocks cool in the broth; and then return the broth to the beans. Remove the meat from the bones and return the meat to the beans or reserve it for use in Macaroni with Beans, Roasted Pumpkin, and Ham Hocks (page 182).

macaroni with beans, roasted pumpkin, and ham hocks

SERVES 8 TO 10

4 cups ½-inch cubed peeled small, sweet orange "eating" pumpkin or winter squash, such as butternut (about 1½ pounds)

3 tablespoons extra virgin olive oil, plus more for serving

Kosher salt and freshly ground black pepper

1 pound dried large macaroni-type pasta

2 large red onions, cut in half and then lengthwise into ¼-inch-thick slices

8 garlic cloves, smashed and coarsely chopped

2 cups shredded cooked ham hock meat

3 dried red chiles, such as de Arbol, crumbled if more heat is desired

Leaves from 3 to 4 small sprigs fresh rosemary (about 2 tablespoons)

¾ cup dry white wine

2 cups cooked white beans

2 cups bean cooking liquid

Grated Parmesan cheese, for serving

Preheat the oven to 475°F. Bring a large heavy pot of salted water to a boil. Place a large heavy baking sheet in the oven for several minutes to preheat. In a large bowl, toss the pumpkin with 1 tablespoon of the oil and a generous sprinkling of salt, and then spread it out in one layer on the hot baking sheet. Return to the oven and roast for about 8 minutes, tossing once about halfway through, until the pumpkin is golden brown but not quite tender. Set aside.

Cook the pasta in the boiling water until it is not quite al dente. Scoop out 3 cups of the cooking water into a bowl before draining the noodles in a colander in the sink; set both aside.

Return the pot to the stove over medium-high heat. Add 1 tablespoon of the oil along with the onion and garlic, tossing to coat them in the oil, and season with salt. Cook for about 3 minutes, until the onion is starting to wilt and get a bit of color. Push the onion to one side and re-center the pot so that the now empty space is over the hottest part of the burner. Add the remaining 1 tablespoon oil and then the ham, chiles, rosemary, and a pinch of salt. Cook for 1 minute, until the ham gets some color and the rosemary and chiles start to crisp. Add the wine and cook for 30 seconds, scraping the pan, until slightly reduced. Raise the heat and add the beans and bean liquid. Bring to a boil and add the pasta, stir well, and cook for 1 minute. Season with salt, and add pasta cooking water as needed to keep about 1½ inches or so of liquid in the bottom of the pot. Add the squash and continue to cook until the squash is hot and cooked through and the pasta is the desired tenderness, about 3 minutes. Add a little extra pasta water if necessary to moisten, and divide among warm bowls, passing the Parmesan cheese and extra olive oil at the table.

old-fashioned baked beans
with smoked bacon

SERVES 6 AS A SIDE DISH

¼ cup tomato paste

¼ cup sorghum (see page 205)

3 tablespoons dry mustard

2 tablespoons cider vinegar

1 tablespoon dark brown sugar

Kosher salt

1 cup dark beer

2 quarts cooked white beans, drained, cooking liquid reserved

6 thick slices smoked bacon

Preheat the oven to 400°F.

In a medium bowl, combine the tomato paste, sorghum, dry mustard, vinegar, brown sugar, and 1 teaspoon salt. Slowly stir in the beer. Add the beans plus enough of their reserved cooking liquid to create a slightly soupy texture. Combine, and taste for salt, adding a bit more if necessary. Reserve the remaining bean cooking liquid. Transfer the mixture to a shallow baking dish and top with the bacon. Bake for 30 to 40 minutes, until the bacon is golden brown and the beans are very hot, checking several times and adding a little more liquid or water if necessary so that the beans don't dry out; they should remain a bit saucy.

OYSTERS

I ate a dozen raw oysters for breakfast at Lantern this morning with Bernie Herman, an amateur oyster farmer and distinguished folklore professor, comparing oysters harvested from two neighboring creeks on Virginia's eastern shore. Bernie has spent the last several years propagating oysters and helping to bring back his own Westerhouse Creek native line. If you don't like oysters, you may assume that we did it for science, but oyster lovers will know that taste tests are always an excuse to eat more oysters.

I give oysters credit for some of my best times. On my first trip to New Orleans, when I was seventeen, my eagle-eyed dad spotted Julia Child getting into a car and convinced our cab driver to chase her all over the Garden District, hoping to introduce me to my idol, ideally embarrassing me in the process. Julia lost us, but we happily ended up at Acme Oyster House and ate as many dozens as only an oyster glutton can with another. And oysters were the center of our favorite party, fifteen years ago at our old house in the country, on my last New Year's Eve outside a restaurant kitchen. The truly devoted spent their night packed into the mudroom under a bare bulb, drinking the Champagne of beers, banging their heads on the low ceiling, and opening bluepoints on a wobbly card table. My obsession has also been a problem. I endangered a close friendship in my crazed, afternoon-long pursuit of an unmarked oyster farm near Point Reys, California, on a winding road in a rainstorm. She wanted to give up and go home, as we had just finished a lunch of the local specialty—barbecued oysters, naturally. But we were so close and there was the hope of raw Hog Island Kumamotos, just out of the sea. If you too feel the pull of the briny deep, did I mention that my friend was nine months pregnant at the time?

Oysters are all about salt, and Stump Sound, just north of Topsail Beach, North Carolina, has to be one of the saltiest estuaries in the South. Bonnie and Jim Schwartzenberg raise their oysters in the waters next to the farmhouse where Bonnie and her six brothers and sisters were born. Unlike many other forms of farm-raised seafood that create pollution in the form of excess feed and waste, filter-feeders like oysters, clams, and mussels actually help clean the waters where they are raised—oysters filter more than fifty gallons of seawater a day—and don't require feed made from wild-caught fish. Jim's main challenge is getting the oyster larvae to "set," or start growing, on their new home: reefs of old oyster shells set deep in the tidal pool. A year and a half later, Jim harvests his "J&B" (for Jim and Bonnie) oysters and thumb-size littleneck clams in a small motorboat, hauling up the nearby flat mesh cages that weigh more than he does. As development increases, the future of oyster farming in Stump Sound is uncertain, but for now we eat all we can.

oyster stew

In a good oyster stew, the oyster liquor is as important as the meat itself: the point is to surround the warm, barely cooked oysters with a rich, briny cream. Use only very fresh, tasty oysters; since the only other ingredients are cream and butter, the stew will only be as flavorful as the oysters themselves. Serve with a stack of crisp hot buttered toast.

SERVES 4

20 salty oysters, freshly shucked and liquor reserved, or 1 pint of the very best shucked
    oysters, with their liquor
1½ cups heavy cream
4 tablespoons (½ stick) unsalted butter, at room temperature
¼ to ½ teaspoon kosher salt, or more as needed depending on the saltiness of the oysters
Pinch of cayenne
Freshly ground black pepper

Strain the oysters, reserving the liquid. Heat the cream in a heavy nonreactive 2-quart pot to a low simmer over medium heat, being careful not to let it scorch. In the meantime, warm four small bowls, add 1 tablespoon of the butter to each bowl, and set them in a warm spot.

    Season the cream with the salt, cayenne, and some black pepper. Add the oyster liquor and return to a simmer. Add the oysters and cook for 30 seconds, until they start to curl and are just heated through. Adjust the seasoning, and divide the oysters and sauce among the warm bowls.

raw oysters on ice with hot sauce

In restaurants, raw oysters tend to be disappointing and expensive. At home they are a slightly messy but relatively cheap treat. Skip the sweet cocktail sauce and serve them with a bottle of good hot sauce—classic and delicious.

SHUCKING OYSTERS

Fishmonger Tom Robinson (see page 54) opens his oysters bare-handed, using a pocket-knife; I prefer a sturdy table and something less sharp. Opening oysters takes a little practice and is more about cautious finesse than brute force; in fact swagger and over-exertion are often what cause injuries. If an oyster is particularly stubborn, try opening it in a different spot or put it aside. Any that prove impossible can be steamed or grilled later.

Soak your oysters in cold water for a few minutes to loosen the dirt. Then scrub them thoroughly with a stiff brush and rinse them under cold running water. Fold a dry kitchen towel once or twice and place it on the edge of a table. Put an oyster on the towel with its hinge facing you and the larger, cupped half of the shell on the bottom. Fold the edge of the towel up over the far end of the oyster and place the heel of your hand firmly on top, securing the oyster to the table and protecting your hand with the towel. With the other hand, hold an oyster knife parallel to the table and slowly but firmly wiggle it into the spot on the hinge that seems to have the most potential for leverage, twisting the knife in one direction and then the other until the oyster pops open. Wipe the blade clean and remove the top shell, keeping the oyster level so the liquor stays in the bottom shell. Wipe the blade again and slide the knife under the oyster to sever the muscle that connects it to its shell. Remove any little bits of shell or dirt. Eat the oyster immediately. If opening a large quantity, set the oysters on a bed of crushed ice or rock salt to keep them level as you go. When he is opening oysters, Tom never stops to put one down; he hands them off until there are no takers and only then eats one himself.

CLAY-POT COOKING

Our fig tree will lose its leaves to frost any day now, so I have been thinking about the meal that I had a few months ago in Santa Cruz, in the backyard of William Rubel, the author of the transformative hearth-cooking book, *The Magic of Fire*. The centerpiece of the meal was chicken thighs larded with rosemary, garlic, and anchovy, wrapped in juicy fig leaves, and then gently cooked in their own fat in a tightly sealed clay pot in his backyard pizza oven. In the steamy mini-oven of the pot, the skin nearly dissolved and combined with the chicken juice into the perfect sauce, a rich contrast to the mysteriously scented leaf. It's a miracle dish, but just typical impromptu nosh for William. It may sound complicated, but—after we lit the fire in his pizza oven with the help of an

industrial flame-thrower—it couldn't have been easier. As the oven heated, I walked with William and his two-year-old, Stella, to the farmers' market, where we wandered around and each grabbed whatever caught our eye: fresh shell beans, padrón peppers, and plums. Back at the house, I automatically headed for the kitchen and its peelers and colanders, but was redirected by William to the sturdy garden table next to the fire to prep for our meal. We poured the contents of our market bags into a few iron pans and clay dishes, adding some oil and a little salt, and pushed them into the back of the oven with a long poker. We snacked and burned our fingers as we pulled the various pans out of the oven, finishing with the chicken, soaking up the juices with flatbreads from the oven.

I was tempting fate trying to re-create that perfect meal indoors in our pizza-oven-less kitchen, but it worked, remarkably well. Since we had several pescatarians in the house, I gave the same treatment to some thick pieces of flounder in its skin and as it all bubbled away in the oven we started off with some smokey red lentil soup.

red lentil soup with smoked paprika

Quick-cooking red lentils have a sweet, mild flavor that pairs well with rich paprika.

SERVES 8 GENEROUSLY, WITH LEFTOVERS

2 tablespoons expeller-pressed vegetable oil

1 medium onion, diced

1 small celery stalk, diced

2 small carrots, diced

1 red bell pepper, diced

Kosher salt and freshly ground black pepper

2 teaspoons hot or sweet smoked paprika, or a combination, to taste

2 teaspoons sweet (unsmoked) paprika

1 teaspoon ground cumin

1 cup dry white wine

2 medium tomatoes, chopped

3 cups red lentils

Large pinch (about 15 threads) of saffron

1 teaspoon sugar

Juice of 1 lemon

Yogurt or crème fraîche (page 224), for serving

Leaves of fresh tender herbs, such as cilantro or dill, for serving

Heat the oil in a large heavy pot over medium heat, and add the onion, celery, carrots, and bell pepper. Reduce the heat, season with salt and pepper, and sauté, stirring frequently, for about 5 minutes, until wilted and starting to color. Add both paprikas and the cumin, and briefly toast until fragrant. Deglaze the pan with the wine, and once it has bubbled away, add the tomatoes, season again with salt, and stir well. Cook until most of the tomato juices have reduced, about 3 minutes.

Add the lentils, 2½ quarts water, the saffron, and the sugar. Bring to a simmer and cook over medium-low heat until the lentils are completely tender, 10 to 15 minutes.

Give the soup a few pulses with an immersion blender to create a creamy but still chunky texture. Add the lemon juice and check the seasoning. Serve with a dollop of yogurt and herb leaves.

clay-pot chicken in fig leaves

Preheat the oven to 350°F. Remove the bones from 8 large skin-on chicken thighs. If you don't live in a figgy climate, rinse some brined grape leaves from a jar.

In a mortar, make a rough paste of rosemary (about ⅓ cup loosely piled leaves), 5 large garlic cloves, a few good anchovy fillets, and dried red chile flakes to taste. If you have had trouble using a mortar and pestle in the past, try using it in tandem with a knife and cutting board: coarsely chop the rosemary (about 2 tablespoons chopped), smash the garlic with the side of a knife and give it a rough chop along with the anchovies, and then combine it all with the chile flakes and a little salt in the mortar, mashing it for 3 or 4 minutes. It can all be done on the board with a knife, but using the mortar will create a magic fragrance and better texture. Add a little olive oil and pound it in to make a coarse, spreadable paste.

Generously season the meat with salt and pepper inside and out, smear an eighth of the paste on the skinless side of each thigh, and roll it into a little bundle, wrapping the skin around to cover as much of the thigh as possible.

Now for the leaves: Fig leaves are shaped like a fat hand. Start by placing a leaf, top side down with the fingers away from you, on a flat surface. Place a chicken bundle, seam side down, at the base of the palm and begin to roll it up, starting with the thumb and pinky and gathering the other fingers snugly, envelope-style, as you go. Place the packets, seam side down, in a lightly oiled clay or cast-iron baking dish, drizzle with a little olive oil, and cover with a tight-fitting lid. Bake in the oven for about 1 hour, or until the chicken is tender and the juices are light pink.

RED LEAVES

Having just tasted one of the deep scarlet grapefruits we got in the mail from L'Hoste this week, I went to the market to buy lettuce today and saw nothing but red—Red Salad Bowl, Flame, and Freckles romaine—along with some buttery sunflower seedlings to mix it up. If you have never had sunflower sprouts, you are in for a treat. Seriously. Succulent and nutty, sunflower sprouts will not at all remind you of a salad you ate in the 1970s or of a refrigerated vegetarian sandwich from a present-day food co-op.

Most farmers have row covers on their greens now to help them make it through the cold nights, and salad is already scarce. This is a nice meaty one and will probably be the last of the year.

red lettuces with blue cheese, red grapefruit, and sunflower sprouts

Gently tear a few small heads of mixed reddish lettuces into bite-size pieces and place them in the bowl of a salad spinner. (I was unconsciously tortured for years by a salad spinner I got in college until my mother-in-law kindly put me out of my misery with a large Oxo. It even has a brake if you are worried your greens might get *too* dry.) Cover the leaves with room-temperature water—or even slightly warm if the lettuces are a little wilted or tired—and allow them to soak for 10 minutes before lifting them out of their bath and spinning them dry.

Using a small, sharp knife, peel a large red grapefruit by carefully slicing the skin away from the fruit, top and bottom first. Then, placing the grapefruit on one of the stable cut ends, slice away the remaining peel, top to bottom, around the sides, leaving just a bit of fruit on the skin in order to completely remove the pith. Hold the peeled fruit over a small bowl, and with a sharp paring knife, carefully remove the segments by slicing along the edge of each crescent-shaped section of fruit as close to the membrane as possible, allowing each piece of pith-free fruit to drop into the bowl.

Squeeze a little lemon juice into a large wooden salad bowl, catching any seeds in your hand. Tip in the accumulated grapefruit juice and add a splash of good-quality white wine vinegar, a big pinch of salt, and a little pinch of sugar. With a fork, whisk in olive oil—about twice as much as the combined vinegar and citrus juices. Add a few grinds of black pepper, and toss with the lettuces. Check the seasoning. Lay the grapefruit sections and trimmed sunflower sprouts on top, along with some chunks of an assertive blue cheese like Bayley Hazen Blue from Jasper Hill Farm in Vermont or Rogue River Blue from Oregon.

MEAT AS A CONDIMENT

Tonight I am trying to feed a vegetarian and a meat-lover whose only common ground might be their hatred of seafood. Late this morning, I was at the farmers' market wishing for different friends so I could just roast a chicken or a fish and be done with it. The discovery of some fresh chicken livers and a big pile of oak-grown shiitakes saved me. I grabbed some white sweet potatoes and apples, too.

Eating less meat has made me a better cook at home and at the restaurant. It has forced me to be less hung up on "center-of-the-plate" items, as the food industry joylessly calls those big, dense portions of meat or fish that we have come to expect from restaurant meals, and to have more flexibility and engagement with food at the market. While meat as the focus of a meal calls for regimented starches and side dishes, starting from an integral flavor of the season—whether woodsy mushrooms in late fall or the tonic of raw greens in the spring—gives an immediate context for "the protein." By using meat and seafood more sparingly, along with real flavor from seasonal ingredients, you're putting your energy and thought where the taste lives.

Meals that use meat or seafood this way may be slightly smaller and end with fewer leftovers but are ultimately more satisfying. One approach treats meat or seafood like a condiment: a rich fish like mackerel added to the skillet to flavor a hash of tender potatoes and sweet sautéed onions, or a spicy cured salami shaved over a soft-cooked egg and steamed asparagus. Tonight's dinner takes a different tack, flipping the typical arrangement by turning the meat into the savory side dish.

white sweet potato soup

SERVES 6 TO 8

2 tablespoons expeller-pressed vegetable oil

3 medium-large yellow onions, thinly sliced (5 cups)

2 tablespoons chopped fresh ginger

4 large garlic cloves, chopped

Kosher salt and freshly ground white pepper

¼ cup dry white wine

2 pounds (about 4) white sweet potatoes, peeled and sliced into ½-inch-thick rounds

½ cup sake

2 tablespoons mirin

½ cup heavy cream

3 tart apples, peeled, quartered, cored, and cut into ½-inch pieces

3 tablespoons sweet white miso

Heat the oil in a heavy 6-quart pot over low heat, and add the onions, ginger, garlic, 1 teaspoon salt, and ¼ teaspoon pepper. Cover and cook slowly until the onions are soft but not browned, 20 minutes or longer.

Add the wine and cook, uncovered, for 5 minutes, until slightly reduced. Add the sweet potatoes, 5 cups water, and the sake, mirin, cream, and 2 teaspoons salt. Cover and simmer until the sweet potatoes are half-tender, about 6 minutes. Add the apples and cook until both the apples and the potatoes are tender, about 10 minutes. Remove from the heat, add the miso, and puree in batches in a blender, or in the pan using an immersion blender. Adjust to the desired thickness with water, and check the seasoning before serving.

warm mushroom salad
with shallots and sherry vinegar

SERVES 4

2 garlic cloves
2 thick slices of bread from a large rustic loaf, lightly toasted
5 tablespoons plus 2 teaspoons extra virgin olive oil
½ pound shiitake mushrooms, stemmed, caps cut into 1-inch-thick slices
Kosher salt and freshly ground black pepper
½ pound oyster mushrooms, trimmed and left whole or broken in half if very large
½ pound button or cremini mushrooms, stemmed and cut in half or quarters if very large
4 shallots, peeled and cut into thin rings
2 cups frisée or thinly sliced endive
½ cup fresh flat-leaf parsley leaves, roughly torn
¼ cup ½-inch batons of fresh chives
1 tablespoon sherry vinegar
Juice of ½ lemon

Preheat the oven to 400°F.

Rub the garlic firmly on both sides of each slice of bread and then break the bread apart into large, rough croutons to make about 25 total. Lay them on a small baking sheet, drizzle with 1 tablespoon of the oil, toss, and toast in the oven for about 5 minutes, until golden brown but still slightly chewy in the middle. Set aside.

Have ready two large, heavy baking sheets. In a medium bowl, toss the shiitakes with 1 tablespoon of the oil, a big pinch of salt, and a grind or two of pepper. Spread them in one layer over half of one of the baking sheets. Repeat the procedure in the same bowl with the oyster mushrooms, arranging them next to the shiitakes, and then the buttons, putting them on the second baking sheet. Season and toss the shallots with the 2 teaspoons oil and salt and pepper, and arrange them alongside the button mushrooms. Roast for about 10 minutes, rotating the pans once during cooking, until the mushrooms are tender and the edges are golden brown. The buttons and shallots will probably take a few minutes longer than the rest.

While the mushrooms and shallots are cooking, toss the frisée, parsley, and chives in a large serving bowl with the sherry vinegar, lemon juice, the remaining 1 tablespoon olive oil, and salt and pepper to taste. When all the mushrooms and the shallots are done, add to the salad along with the croutons.

pan-roasted chicken livers with thyme and schmaltz

A jar of rendered golden chicken fat, or schmaltz, is a faithful friend in the kitchen—tossed with noodles and toasted bread crumbs, added to dumplings in chicken broth, or smeared on flatbread with herbs before baking. These livers are a good companion to a hearty vegetable dish like the Warm Mushroom Salad (page 198).

SERVES 4 AS PART OF A LARGER MEAL

1 pound chicken livers, trimmed and patted dry just before cooking
1 teaspoon kosher salt
3 tablespoons chicken fat (olive oil may be substituted, but keep the heat lower—below the smoking point)
Handful of fresh thyme leaves
Flaky sea salt, such as Maldon
Freshly ground black pepper

Heat a 9-inch or larger cast-iron skillet over high heat for 1 minute. Have nearby a lid large enough to cover the pan, to extinguish a possible flare-up and protect you from momentary splattering.

Season the livers with the kosher salt. Add the chicken fat to the pan, and then add the livers all at once, quickly spreading them out in one layer with tongs. Scatter the thyme around the livers (don't move them yet), pushing it down so that it cooks in the fat. If the livers are not cooking evenly, rotate the pan itself instead of moving the livers. Continue to cook over high heat for 2 minutes, until the edges of the livers are crispy and deep golden brown. Flip the livers over with tongs and cook for another 30 seconds to 1 minute for medium-rare. Transfer them to a warm platter along with the thyme, and sprinkle with sea salt and freshly ground black pepper.

SNOW-DAY FOOD

It's a bright gray morning and so cold that we had to dig out the bag of mittens—never before seen by Arthur—from storage. It looks a little like snow, and I join the kids in hoping for a real storm, but snow-day food is more realistic: I'm thinking about my grandmother's savory pot roast with lots of gravy.

It may come as no surprise to learn that a woman who used family-size bags of Utz potato chips as packing material in a box of presents to her grandchildren also made an excellent pot roast. Christmas morning was a party, not in celebration of the toys and hand-sewn outfits she had sent but of the showers of lard-fried chips. From homemade scrapple to apple dumplings, my grandma Marie cooked with the same resourceful hands that packed those boxes. Driving to her house in Lancaster, Pennsylvania, from New Jersey, we played our own dinnertime car bingo; you scored by accurately predicting the precise number of pickles or exactly which cold cuts or casseroles might greet us on her "boo-fay," a twenty-foot-long shuffleboard table she had bought from the neighborhood bar when it closed. She constructed a plywood top to protect the polished gaming surface from the longest parade of food seen outside the Mount Joy Legion Hall. The next room was our grandpa Al's gaming domain: a dartboard and a Ping-Pong table that was sometimes turned over to the jugs and plastic tubes and siphons Marie used to make her dandelion wine, fermented from flowers that Al had foraged—with greater enthusiasm once he was affected by Alzheimer's—from neighborhood lawns.

Marie was generous with neighbors and sometimes sly; on summer nights, once the water was boiling in her biggest pot, she would send the kids across the road to pick corn from the neighboring farmer's vast field, assuring us that the deer would eat more that night than we would. She had raised her family in the city, but even when she moved to a house with a big backyard of her own for vegetables, she kept her ten-foot-square plot in the community garden, preferring the patchwork of crops and families who hauled water together and weeded in the evenings after work. My dad keeps a jar of his mom's 1977 green beans in his pantry, and I have heard family rumors of early 1980s sauerkraut and brandied cherries. I wish I had a jar of her bread-and-butter pickles.

pot roast with gravy

Marie called most any dish that she added wine to "French," and her French pot roast was a star of the genre. The paprika and bell pepper are additions from the late writer Laurie Colwin, who along with Marie would top my list of people to eat pot roast with.

SERVES 8 TO 10

1 (4-pound) boneless beef chuck roast, preferably grass-fed

Kosher salt and freshly ground black pepper

2 tablespoons expeller-pressed vegetable oil

2 thick pieces of smoked slab bacon, roughly chopped

1 large onion, sliced

1 large carrot, sliced

1 celery stalk, sliced

4 garlic cloves, smashed and peeled

1 red bell pepper, sliced

¼ cup sweet paprika

2 dried bay leaves

1 cup fruity red wine

1 (28-ounce) can peeled tomatoes, with juice

Season the roast generously with salt and pepper, preferably 24 hours in advance, and refrigerate.

If the roast is floppy or tapered, tie it into a compact shape with kitchen twine. Allow it to come to room temperature, about 1 hour.

Preheat the oven to 300°F.

Heat a large, heavy Dutch oven (this dish has a tendency to age a pot's interior; if possible pick a pot that has already been well used) over medium-low heat. Add the oil and then the roast. Sear the meat on all sides, turning it frequently, until it is deep golden brown and all the fat is rendered, about 20 minutes. Set the roast aside on a plate.

Add the bacon to the pot and cook it over medium heat until it softens and starts to turn translucent, about 1 minute. Then add the onion, carrot, celery, garlic, and bell pepper, season with salt and pepper, and sauté for 2 to 3 minutes, until the vegetables have softened. Add the paprika, lower the heat a bit, and cook for another few minutes, until it darkens to

RECIPE CONTINUES

a deeper red and is very fragrant. Add the bay leaves and wine, simmer for 2 minutes, and then add the tomatoes along with their juice, gently squeezing each one over the pot with your fingers to break them up as they go in. Return the mixture to a simmer for a minute or so, adding a little more salt if necessary.

Return the roast to the pot, and as the liquid returns to a low simmer, spoon some over the vegetables and the meat to moisten it. Place a piece of parchment or aluminum foil on top of the meat and then crimp it snugly around the roast so that the edges nearly meet the liquid. Cover the pot with a tight-fitting lid, transfer it to the oven, and braise for about 3 hours, turning the roast over once or twice during this time, until the meat is very tender.

Transfer the roast to a carving board and discard the bay leaves. Use an immersion blender to puree the gravy in the pot, or better yet, push it through a coarse sieve with a spatula. Remove the kitchen twine if necessary, slice the roast, and serve with the warm gravy.

glazed carrots

If you are using larger carrots, cut them into 2- to 3-inch batons.

SERVES 8 TO 10

8 tablespoons (1 stick) unsalted butter
2 pounds small carrots, 3 to 6 inches long, trimmed and quartered lengthwise
    unless very small
1 tablespoon kosher salt
Large pinch of sugar
2 tablespoons Pernod or other anise-flavored liqueur

In a large, heavy sauté pan, melt 6 tablespoons of the butter. Add the carrots and enough water to cover them halfway. Season with the salt, sugar, and Pernod. Place a lid on the pan and cook over very low heat for 8 to 10 minutes, until the carrots are almost tender. Remove the lid and continue to cook for a few minutes more, gently tossing, until the liquid has nearly evaporated. Remove from the heat, swirl in the remaining 2 tablespoons butter, and adjust the seasoning before serving.

sour cream ice cream with sorghum

Sorghum is a rich, earthy syrup produced mostly in the South and Midwest from a naturally sweet and juicy grass of the same name. So nutritious that doctors used to recommend a daily dose, it is similar to molasses but a little less sweet and with a deeper flavor.

MAKES ABOUT 3 QUARTS

4 cups sour cream or crème fraîche, homemade (page 224) or store-bought
4 cups (1 quart) buttermilk
2½ cups sugar
Sorghum or dark molasses, for serving

Whisk together the sour cream, buttermilk, and sugar until the sugar dissolves. Freeze in an ice cream maker.

Serve immediately, drizzled with sorghum, or pack into a container, cover, and freeze for up to 3 days.

winter

GATHERING NUTS PAGE 210
Roasted Chestnuts in the Fireplace

CITRUS FROM THE BAYOU PAGE 212
Ruby Grapefruit Cordial
Roast Moulard Duck with Kumquats and
Salt-Cured Chiles
Juicy Satsuma Orange Cake

TOUGH LOVE: WINTER GREENS PAGE 219
Turnip and Mustard Greens with Smoked Bacon
and Vinegar
Slow-Cooked Black Kale with Stewed Garlic
Kale Panini
Instant Spinach
Colcannon with Scallions and Greens

"PANTRY" MEALS PAGE 225
Steamed Black Cod and Potatoes with Pounded
Parsley, Garlic, and Mussels
Crispy Chicken with Rye Bread, Mustard,
and Sweet and Sour Red Cabbage
Whole Roasted Onions

THE BEE'S KNEES PAGE 231
Honey Frozen Custard with Honeycomb Candy

FAMILY MEAL PAGE 235

Miguel Torres's Carnitas

Jalapeño and Red Onion Escabeche

Green Cabbage Salad

Salsa Verde

Salsa Roja

HOMELY VEGETABLES PAGE 241

Turnip Soup with Rosemary and Black Pepper

Sautéed Savoy Cabbage with Speck and Lemon

Roasted Japanese Turnips with Honey

Choucroute Garnie 1-2-3

Curried Beets

OVERNIGHT COOKING PAGE 249

Overnight Pot-on-Fire

Onion-Braised Overnight Brisket

COOK IT WHOLE PAGE 253

Roast Chicken with Fennel and Spring Onions

No-Poach Poached Chicken

Roasted Spareribs with Crushed Fennel and Red Chiles

WATERCRESS FROM A STREAM PAGE 260

Watercress with a Fried Egg and Black Sesame Sauce

GATHERING NUTS

Arthur has been singing "The Christmas Song" ("chestnuts roasting on an open fire . . .") for a full year now, and this afternoon it has finally occurred to me to actually roast some. (Year-round holiday singing seems to run in the family; when Oona was three, her bedtime song was "Frosty the Snowman," every verse, every night.) Mac already has a fire going and I found a bottle of Lambrusco that reminds me of the "Cold Duck" (sweet, bubbly wine) my grandma used to make.

These chestnuts are fairly soft, moist, and easy to peel. I put them in an iron pan, rake some embers into a pile on the side of the fire, and place the pan on top, stirring every so often. Twenty minutes later, the shells are black-brown and have curled open to expose the yellow nut. The living room smells like sweet caramel, marshmallow, and smoke, the same aroma of the chestnuts that we ate a few weeks ago in Kyoto, roasted at 800 degrees in what looked like a pressurized cannon (the nuts were blistered, sweet, and easy to peel), or many years ago in Zurich, where women wrapped in mink lined up at a smoking cart to purchase chestnuts wrapped in a newspaper cone, or the ones I first tried with my parents in Chinatown in the 1970s (roasted over charcoal, but for me still a future acquired taste). Oona eats one and decides she loves the smell, but not so much the nut, and Arthur takes a pass, excited enough just to see his song in action. We have lots left over to make chestnut soup with sautéed Jerusalem artichokes, and a chestnut pudding for dessert.

At the turn of the century, one out of every four hardwood trees in the Appalachians was an American chestnut. In early summer, from Maine to Mississippi, the dense white blossoms covering the crowns of the often eighty-foot-tall trees created the appearance of just-fallen snow, and in western North Carolina, the moment was known as Christmas in July. The American chestnut started to succumb to a terrible blight in the early 1900s and by the 1950s was nearly extinct.

Our chestnuts at Lantern come from High Rock Farm, a former stagecoach stop where Richard Teague planted his Dunstan trees—a hybrid bred from a hardy American chestnut survivor found in the 1950s and Chinese varieties—in 1991; they are now thirty feet tall.

In late fall, Richard harvests thousands of pounds of chestnuts from his farm, where he also cultivates twenty acres of pecans, blackberries, and sweet cherries. For the last twenty-seven years, biologists working with the American Chestnut Foundation have been developing and testing a new disease-resistant hybrid that is even closer genetically to the original American—down to its massive size, beautiful open leaf pattern, and sweet nuts—that will finally be ready for planting within a few years. Since chestnuts trees grow up to four times as quickly as oaks, the prospect of a mass reforestation has a tremendous, if somewhat fantastic, appeal from a global warming perspective. However, it does seem possible that fifty years from now, American chestnuts could be back—maybe in some forests, but certainly in orchards—and that by then today's kids will be hungry for them.

roasted chestnuts in the fireplace

There are chestnut roasting devices—long-handled iron skillets or perforated baskets that allow the flames direct contact with the nuts—but they are not necessary; any way you can get the chestnuts in a hot fire and close to the flames works well. Chestnuts are high in

moisture—more like a fruit than a nut—and fairly perishable. Look for nuts that are dark brown, shiny, and heavy and store them in the refrigerator.

Using a small sharp knife, score an X across the soft end of each nut—or if you find it easier, on the side of the nut. Soak them in cold water for 10 minutes; then drain and dry well. Put the nuts in an iron skillet over embers in a hot part of a fireplace (or directly on the grate of a hot charcoal grill or on a sheet pan in a preheated 450°F oven) and toss frequently until the shells blacken in spots and are crisp and easy to peel, about 20 minutes. They stay warm in a few layers of tea towels for nearly an hour. If you have leftovers, peel while they are still warm.

CITRUS FROM THE BAYOU

Oona and Arthur had their own New Year's Eve bash with friends last night, and when we walked in at 3 a.m. after our own long night, their sitter cheerfully told us that they had all just gone to bed. This morning, it's glasses of fresh, tart juice all around: grapefruit for groggy grown-ups and tangerine for the kids, who were only a few hours shy of their goal of staying up until the sunrise.

In late November, when winter suddenly feels like it's actually going to happen, we get our first shipment of citrus from Linda and Lester L'Hoste's citrus farm in Plaquemines Parish, Louisiana. The first box is filled with satsuma oranges, full of bright acid but candy-sweet and perfectly balanced. Shipments of ruby grapefruit, kumquats, Meyer lemons, limes, mandarins, navels, tangelos, and tangerines then arrive every two weeks or so until the end of February.

When the L'Hostes transitioned to organic farming methods in 1995, they bought a million ladybugs, whose descendants still live with other helpful insects in the knee-high native nutgrass that forms paths between the rows of trees, about 2,000 in all. Occasionally the grass is cut and left on the ground as mulch that decomposes and adds life to their soil—a recent measurement showed that the L'Hostes' earth contains four times more organic matter than a typical conventional system. When they had insect problems before they went organic, the L'Hostes would spray. Now, they only rarely see the bugs that plagued them and usually when they do, the bugs don't cause the same kind of damage here as they do on neighboring citrus farms, where herbicides knock down the grass but render the soil practically sterile.

Tasting L'Hoste's fruit convinced me to stop eating citrus out of season, holding back to enjoy it as compensation for winter. Eating one of their satsumas is a reminder that kids used to actually thank Santa for putting an orange at the bottom of their stockings. At Lantern, L'Hoste fruit arrives just in time to replace the last, battered shreds of summer and fall on our menu with warm, spicy kumquats with juicy roast duck; a grapefruit salad with fresh lemongrass for caramelized sea scallops; salty, pungent Indian-style spicy lime pickle with a garlicky chickpea puree; a tempura of thinly sliced Meyer lemon and sweet leeks; and bowls of blood orange "creamsicle" ice cream and grapefruit sherbet. At home, we eat each new fruit from Louisiana fresh for the first week or so then start cooking it: lemon relish on hot, crispy flounder fillets; fresh sweet orange peel added to a beef stew; and satsumas glazed on a juicy, buttery cake.

ruby grapefruit cordial

SERVES 6 TO 8

1 cup sugar
½ cup dried elderflowers (see Sources, page 264)
Pinch of kosher salt
6 cups freshly squeezed pink grapefruit juice, or to taste, chilled

In a small saucepan, bring 1 cup water to a boil. Remove from the heat and immediately add the sugar, salt, and elderflowers, stirring until the sugar is completely dissolved. Let steep for 10 minutes and then strain. Let cool. Combine with the grapefruit juice to taste, and serve chilled or over ice.

roast moulard duck
with kumquats and salt-cured chiles

SERVES 4

1 (2-pound) moulard duck breast

2 teaspoons Spice Cure (recipe follows)

2 tablespoons expeller-pressed vegetable oil

8 garlic cloves, smashed and peeled

1 (2-inch) piece of fresh ginger, cut into very fine julienne

2 tablespoons rice wine

¼ cup plus 2 tablespoons dry white wine

1½ cups Dark Poultry Stock (page 177)

1½ teaspoons sugar

½ teaspoon kosher salt

Diced Salt-Cured Chiles (page 140), to taste

Juice of 1 clementine or tangerine

1 teaspoon cornstarch mixed with 1 teaspoon water

12 sour kumquats, sliced into ¼-inch-thick rounds and seeded (about 1 cup)

Trim the silverskin from the meat. Score the duck skin with a sharp knife, making ⅛-inch shallow incisions about ¼ inch apart. (It is best to do this while the duck is cold.) Pat the duck dry with a paper towel. Season the meat (not skin) side of the duck with the spice cure, making sure not to get any on the skin. (The sugar will burn during cooking.) Put the duck on a plate, skin side down, cover, and refrigerate for at least 6 hours or overnight.

Heat a cast-iron skillet over medium heat and add 1 tablespoon of the oil. When the skillet is hot, put the duck, skin side down, into the pan. Cook over medium heat for about 3 minutes, until the fat starts to render. Reduce the heat to low and cook for another 20 minutes, rotating the duck in the pan as needed to ensure even cooking, until the skin is amber brown and crispy and most of the fat has rendered. Raise the heat to medium. Turn the duck over and cook for another 3 to 4 minutes, until slightly browned. Transfer the duck to a warm platter and let it rest in a warm place for 5 minutes before slicing.

While the duck is cooking, make the sauce: Heat a nonreactive sauté pan over medium heat and add the remaining 1 tablespoon oil. Add the garlic and cook, stirring, for 3 to 4 minutes, until fragrant and golden. Add the ginger. Raise the heat to high and cook for

RECIPE CONTINUES

a minute, until the ginger is fragrant but not browned. Add the rice wine and the white wine, and simmer for 1 to 2 minutes, until the liquid has reduced by about half. Add the stock, sugar, salt, and chiles and bring to a simmer. Reduce the heat to medium and cook for 2 to 3 minutes. Add the citrus juice, stir in the cornstarch mixture, and add the kumquats. Bring back to a simmer, stir until slightly thickened, about 20 minutes, and remove from the heat. Taste for salt, and discard the garlic if desired.

Slice the duck breast into ½-inch-thick slices. Arrange on warm plates, and spoon the sauce over the duck.

spice cure

This cure also works well for duck confit and to flavor roast pork. It keeps in a sealed container for several weeks. Homemade dried tangerine peel can be made in a few days by leaving fresh peel in a warm, dry spot.

MAKES ALMOST I CUP

1 (1-inch) piece of cassia or cinnamon stick
2 silver dollar–size pieces of dried tangerine peel (available in Asian markets)
2 star anise
1 teaspoon Sichuan peppercorns
1 medium red dried chile
½ cup kosher salt
¼ cup sugar

Put the cassia, tangerine peel, star anise, peppercorns, and chile in a spice grinder and process until evenly ground. Transfer to a small bowl and stir in the salt and sugar.

juicy satsuma orange cake

SERVES 8 TO 10

ORANGES AND GLAZE

5 satsuma oranges

Juice of ½ lemon

1 cup sugar

¼ teaspoon kosher salt

CAKE

8 tablespoons (1 stick) unsalted butter, at room temperature, plus more
   for greasing the pan

¾ cup sugar

2 large eggs, at room temperature

⅓ cup semolina flour

⅔ cup all-purpose flour

1 teaspoon baking powder

¼ teaspoon table salt

Preheat the oven to 375°F. Butter a 10-inch round pan.

Finely grate the zest one of the oranges, and reserve the zest for the cake batter. Cut the orange in half, juice it, and strain the juice; you should have ⅓ cup juice. Slice the remaining 4 oranges into ¼-inch-thick rounds. Combine the orange juice, lemon juice, sugar, salt, and orange slices in a medium nonreactive saucepan, and bring to a slow simmer over low heat. Cook for 6 to 7 minutes, until the centers of the orange slices are starting to become tender and translucent but are not falling apart. Carefully transfer the orange slices to a plate with a slotted spoon, and continue to simmer the syrup until it has reduced to ½ cup, 5 to 8 minutes. Set the glaze aside.

To make the cake, combine the butter and sugar in an electric mixer fitted with the paddle attachment and mix until fluffy. While the mixer is running, add an egg and wait for it to be incorporated before adding the other. Add the reserved grated orange zest. In a bowl, sift together the semolina flour, all-purpose flour, baking powder, and salt. Add the flour mixture, a little at a time, to the batter mixture and mix until all of it is incorporated. Pour the batter into the pan and arrange the orange slices in one layer on top of the batter. Bake for 15 minutes.

RECIPE CONTINUES

Reduce the oven temperature to 350°F and bake for 35 to 40 minutes, until the cake is an even golden brown and baked through; a toothpick inserted in the center should come out clean. Let the cake cool on a wire rack until it is warm. Then, using a wooden skewer, poke holes all over the surface of the cake. Brush the glaze over the top, using a pastry brush. Allow the cake to cool to room temperature, and then unmold.

TOUGH LOVE: WINTER GREENS

Driving home from work tonight, late and hungry, I remember that there is not much in the house to eat: two oversize bunches of kale, a few tiny eggs from Monica's young chickens that just started laying, and some Parmesan cheese. Until recently, the discovery would have sent me into a take-out dinner U-turn or at least darkened my mood, but instead I keep going.

Is anyone born loving spinach or craving kale? Not me, but I always tried to do my part, eating collards alongside hoppin' John, steaming spinach for health-conscious guests, and finishing my kale whenever it was served. I ate enough greens not to seem childish, but no more. When I joined George O'Neal's farm share, my "just enough" approach finally met a worthy opponent.

Farm shares, or CSAs (Community Supported Agriculture), is a model in which customers share in the risks and rewards of farming by purchasing a share of the future harvest from a small farm for the growing season. A membership with George's Lil' Farm can include a cup of fresh press-pot coffee when you pick up at the market and a weekly stream-of-consciousness e-mail. The newsy letter has recipes, puns (after a big storm "all hail breaks loose"), pleas ("return your egg cartons!"), and philosophy (on fleeting Dutch irises: "Love them, but don't get attached: this isn't that kind of relationship"). Membership also includes a lot of hearty greens.

Many farms work hard to include a variety of produce each week and design their weekly produce box to look like a square meal: trading with neighbors for crops they don't grow, overwintering carrots, or keeping a row of strawberries in a greenhouse. George delights in a different kind of bounty that dares members to cook at his pace: early spring is a parade of potatoes, July is all about the lily family—garlic, onions, and leeks—and in late summer our share seems to have at least one of each of the thirty varieties of tomatoes he grows. All of this is very welcome, but Lil' Farm's motto (and T-shirt logo) is "Kale 'Em All," a riff on the Metallica album *Kill 'Em All*. Sure enough, this fall, every week I was handed more kale than I ate in a year—regular curly, frilly pink Red Russian, flat "black," or Lacinato. My haul wouldn't even fit in the refrigerator—it was cook or compost.

Under pressure to use it up, I started putting the kale at the center of the plate; I braised it with leeks and tossed it with a little pasta; used it as a filling for a crunchy panini with cheese and pickled chiles; and made it the base of a stew with white beans and spicy sausage. My breakthrough was all about fat; I realized I had been consigning leafy greens to "healthy" side dish territory. I had hung onto childhood feelings, treating greens ascetically—steaming or wilting them all alone—rather than uncovering their richness with cheese, a nutty oil, eggs, mashed potatoes, or smoky bacon.

Dinner tonight is black kale. I rip the leaves off the stems and soak them in a bowl of water while I put a small pot of water on the stove to poach a few of Monica's eggs and grate the Parmesan cheese. When the garlic I've cooked in a skillet with some olive oil is sizzling and soft, the wet kale goes in the pan with a big pinch of salt and then slowly cooks down to a pillow of sweet, dark green leaves. I pile the kale into big warm bowls, lay the poached eggs on top, and follow that with cheese and a long drizzle of olive oil. After all, we are having kale for dinner.

turnip and mustard greens with smoked bacon and vinegar

SERVES 4 AS A SIDE DISH

3 big bunches (about 1½ pounds) mixed mustard and turnip greens
2 teaspoons expeller-pressed vegetable oil or extra virgin olive oil
2 thick slices smoked bacon, cut into ½-inch pieces
1 onion, halved and sliced lengthwise
Kosher salt
Vinegar from pickled chile peppers (see page 141)

Wash the greens, remove the thick stalks, and coarsely chop the leaves.

Heat a large sauté pan over medium heat and add the oil and bacon. Cook the bacon until it is about halfway rendered and still soft, 4 to 5 minutes. Add the onion and season with salt. Cook for 5 to 6 minutes, until the onion is fragrant, translucent, and beginning to turn golden. Add the greens and a big pinch of salt, lower the heat, cover, and cook, stirring occasionally, for about 15 minutes, until the greens are very soft and the water from the greens has evaporated. Adjust the seasoning and serve with the spicy vinegar.

slow-cooked black kale
with stewed garlic

SERVES 2 AS A MAIN COURSE OR 4 AS A SIDE DISH

2 bunches (about 1 pound) of black kale (also known as Lacinato or dinosaur kale),
    stemmed and torn into big pieces
3 tablespoons olive oil
4 garlic cloves, thinly sliced
Kosher salt
½ small dried ancho chile, or to taste, crumbled
3 long strips of lemon zest

Fill a medium-size heavy pot with water and bring it to a boil over high heat. Salt it
generously, add the kale, and blanch for 1 minute. Immediately drain and squeeze dry.

    Return the pot to the stove over low heat, add the olive oil and garlic, season with a
pinch of salt, and cook gently for 3 to 5 minutes, until the garlic is soft but not browned. Add
the chile and let it lightly toast for a moment before adding the kale and lemon zest. Season
with another pinch of salt. Cover and cook over low heat for about 30 minutes, stirring
occasionally and adding a tablespoon or two of water as needed to keep it slightly moist.

kale panini

Billy Cotter devised this delicious meaty sandwich for his vegetarian wife, Kelli, at their restaurant Toast, in downtown Durham.

SERVES 4

2 big bunches of curly kale (about 1 pound total), stemmed, leaves torn into pieces

1½ teaspoons kosher salt

1 tablespoon olive oil, plus more for grilling

1 tablespoon red wine vinegar

8 slices rustic sandwich bread

10 ounces farmer's cheese or other crumbly fresh cheese, such as queso blanco or feta, broken into chunks

Pickled Chile Peppers (page 141)

Freshly ground black pepper

Working in batches, blanch the kale in boiling salted water for 3 minutes, until tender. Use a slotted spoon to transfer each batch to a colander. When all the kale is cooked, let it cool and then squeeze with your hands to remove the excess moisture. Cut the kale into ½-inch-wide strips and put them in a bowl.

Preheat a panini press, or heat a large cast-iron skillet over low heat and have another pan of the same size ready to weight down the sandwiches.

Right before you are ready to assemble the sandwiches, season the kale with salt. Add the oil and toss well. Finish with the vinegar.

Lay out 4 slices of the bread and top them with equal parts kale and cheese; add chiles to taste. Season with salt and pepper, and top with the other slices of bread.

Lightly oil the panini press and follow the manufacturer's instructions for grilling the sandwiches. (If using a pan on the stovetop, raise the heat to medium, lightly oil it, and add as many sandwiches as can comfortably fit. Place the other heavy pan on top to press the sandwiches; if the pan is relatively light, add some weight to it, such as a large can or a full tea kettle. Rotating the pan on the burner frequently, cook the sandwiches for about 5 minutes, until deep golden brown. Transfer the sandwiches to a plate, re-oil the pan, and return the sandwiches to the pan, browned side up, to cook the other side, about 3 minutes.)

instant spinach

SERVES 2

1 pound spinach leaves, preferably Savoy, tough stems removed
2 tablespoons olive oil
2 teaspoons fresh lemon juice
1 teaspoon kosher salt
Freshly ground black pepper

Pile the spinach in a large bowl that will fit into your microwave oven. Cook it in the microwave on high power for 25 to 30 seconds, until it is just warm but not wilted. Toss the spinach with the oil, lemon juice, salt, and pepper to taste. Cook for 30 to 60 seconds, until the spinach is wilted and its volume has reduced by less than half. It will be hot but not so cooked that it starts to throw off liquid.

colcannon with scallions and greens

Colcannon is a traditional Irish dish of boiled potatoes mashed with green onions, leeks or sometimes chives, kale or cabbage, and milk or cream. I like mine extremely green, with lots of black pepper.

SERVES 6 TO 8

2 pounds small Yukon Gold potatoes, well scrubbed
3 big bunches (about 1½ pounds) mixed greens, such as kale or cabbage
12 small scallions, or 3 to 4 larger bulbing spring onions, white and green parts, thinly sliced
1 to 2 cups whole milk, to taste, heated
4 tablespoons (½ stick) unsalted butter, at room temperature
3 tablespoons crème fraîche, store-bought or homemade (recipe follows)
Kosher salt and freshly ground black pepper

Steam the potatoes in a vegetable steamer for about 20 minutes, until tender. Set them aside to cool slightly.

Meanwhile, bring a large pot of salted water to a boil. Stem the greens and blanch the leaves in the boiling water until tender, about 3 minutes. Drain, and cool under cold running water. Drain well, wringing out the excess water with your hands. Finely chop the greens.

When the potatoes are just cool enough to handle but still warm, peel them and then mash them coarsely in a large bowl. Add the greens and scallions. Stir in the hot milk to the desired consistency. Add the butter and crème fraîche, and season with salt and pepper.

crème fraîche

Crème fraîche is just homemade sour cream and is simple to make.

In a bowl, whisk together 1 part buttermilk with 8 parts non-ultra-pasteurized (and preferably non-homogenized) heavy cream. Cover with a cloth or plastic wrap, and leave it out on the counter for 24 to 48 hours, until it thickens. Whisk again before storing, tightly covered, in the refrigerator, where it will keep for several weeks; it gets thicker and more delicious as it ages. Crème fraîche has a higher fat content than commercial sour cream and so can be heated without breaking.

"PANTRY" MEALS

Predictions for snow have been flying thick all week, but before we take them seriously, it's coming down in big, wet flakes and by dawn it's sticking. Oona is reading *Farmer Boy*, Laura Ingalls Wilder's tale of a year in her future husband's boyhood in northern New York State in the 1860s. It's full of head-spinning ideas: breaking colts, shearing sheep, bathing in a washtub by the fire, and fried apples'n'onions. Oona is most awed by the same thing that struck me when I first read it: without a grocery store, the Wilders lead a life that is almost hedonistic, at least at the table. They eat endlessly, all winter long: cracklin' corn bread, crabapple jelly, stacked pancakes, plump sausage cakes, fried doughnuts, baked beans with pork, chicken pie, roast beef with brown gravy, and bird's-nest pudding with thick cream and nutmeg. And with the exception of fresh dairy, it is all pulled from their freezer-attic, root cellar, pickle barrels, and cupboards.

Few cooking projects are as satisfying as making a decent meal from things that are already around, no trip to the store required. Success is a feat of imagination, faith, and, of course, a deep pantry full of things like tinned anchovies, canned tomatoes, dried mushrooms, fish sauce, rice, beans, cornmeal, and dried beans. The kitchen cabinet challenge is great entertainment, but the real value in pantry cooking is not to survive for months, but for just days, or even a week at a time, without much planning or shopping. The less often I have to go to the store in winter, the more time I have to cook at home.

So I extend the idea of what counts as "pantry" to the refrigerator: hearty vegetables and fruits, like carrots, apples, citrus, turnips, beets, and cabbages that keep for weeks; thick, succulent winter lettuces like escarole, endive, and frisée; resilient herbs, like rosemary and parsley (stored like a bouquet in a jar of water); dried sausage and ham hocks; hard cheeses. The vegetable bin below the kitchen counter holds garlic, onions, shallots, and potatoes, and the freezer is stocked with meat and fish, but also nuts, bread crumbs, field peas, bacon, and stocks. Fresh farm eggs keep perfectly for a few weeks, and other slow-perishing perishables, like cream, also expand the possibilities.

Now in the midst of what qualifies here as a snow emergency—eight inches by dinnertime; school will be closed for a week—we know we should have gone to the store, at least for candles. Last night, we had mussels for dinner and there are a few left. There are some fillets of rich sable (also known as black cod), a fatty fish that freezes well. For dinner we steam the sable with some small potatoes and serve it with mussels and broth enriched with pounded parsley and garlic. After doing the dishes, we take stock of what else is in the "pantry" for the coming days.

steamed black cod and potatoes with pounded parsley, garlic, and mussels

SERVES 4

4 cups loosely packed, fresh flat-leaf parsley leaves (from about 1 bunch)

4 small garlic cloves

Kosher salt

2 pounds mussels, scrubbed

12 small potatoes

4 (6-ounce) fillets of black cod (black sable), skin on

Expeller-pressed vegetable oil

Freshly ground black pepper

3 tablespoons unsalted butter

Chop the parsley very fine. Smash the garlic, chop it just a little to make grinding easier, and then work it into a paste with a small pinch of salt in a mortar. Add the parsley and continue to work the mixture in the mortar until smooth.

In a 4-quart pot, bring 2 cups water to a boil, lightly salt it, and add the mussels. Cover and cook over high heat for 3 to 5 minutes, checking the mussels often and transferring them to a plate as soon as they open. Discard any that do not open. Strain the mussel broth through a fine-mesh sieve and reserve it. Shuck half of the mussels.

Set a large steamer basket over a pot filled with a couple of inches of boiling water, and add the potatoes. Cover and cook until the potatoes are close to halfway done, 4 minutes. Meanwhile, drizzle the fish with oil, season it with salt and pepper, and put it on a plate that will fit in the steamer basket, making sure the fillets do not touch each other.

When the potatoes are almost halfway done, add the plate of fish to the steamer basket, and steam for about 6 minutes, until the fish is barely cooked through and the tip of a sharp knife inserted in the thickest part of the fish for 5 seconds comes out warm to the touch. Transfer the fish and potatoes to a warm platter and cover to keep warm.

In a large, deep sauté pan, bring the reserved mussel liquid to a simmer. Add the parsley mixture and cook for 45 seconds. Remove from the heat, add the shucked and unshucked mussels, stir to reheat, and swirl in the butter. Add salt if necessary before spooning the mixture over the fish and potatoes.

crispy chicken with rye bread, mustard, and sweet and sour red cabbage

SERVES 4

1 loaf (about 1 pound) stale rye bread
1½ tablespoons caraway seeds
4 teaspoons kosher salt
2½ teaspoons freshly ground black pepper
8 small boneless, skinless chicken thighs
2 cups all-purpose flour
2 large eggs, beaten
Expeller-pressed vegetable oil
Mustard Sauce (recipe follows)
Sweet and Sour Red Cabbage (recipe follows)

Remove the crust from the bread and tear the bread into bite-size chunks. Grind the chunks, in batches, in a coffee grinder or food processor until it is more or less uniformly ground but still coarse. Spread the crumbs on a baking sheet and let them dry out at room temperature for at least 2 hours (or put them in a 250°F oven for 20 minutes). Measure out 6 cups of crumbs into a large bowl, and add the caraway seeds, 1 teaspoon of the salt, and 1 teaspoon of the pepper.

Heat one or more large cast-iron skillets over medium-high heat. Season the chicken with 2½ teaspoons of the salt and 1 teaspoon of the pepper. Mix the flour in a bowl with the remaining ½ teaspoon salt and ½ teaspoon pepper. Dip each piece of chicken in the flour, shake off any excess, and then dip in the beaten egg. Make sure each piece gets thoroughly covered with egg. Dredge the chicken pieces one by one in the bread crumbs, shaking off any excess.

Swirl 3 tablespoons oil into the hot skillet. Lay as many pieces of chicken in the pan as will comfortably fit, and lower the heat. Cook, rotating the chicken and the pan frequently, for 4 to 5 minutes, until the chicken is dark golden brown. Flip the chicken and add another 1 tablespoon oil. Cook for another 4 to 5 minutes, until the chicken is crispy, golden brown, and cooked through. If at any point the pan seems too dry and the bread crumbs start to burn, add a little more oil. Serve with mustard sauce and cabbage.

mustard sauce

SERVES 4

¼ cup good-quality Dijon mustard
¼ cup chicken stock, preferably homemade (page 177), or water
Big pinch of kosher salt

Whisk together the mustard, stock, and salt, and heat in a small nonreactive saucepan until just hot.

sweet and sour red cabbage

SERVES 4 GENEROUSLY

1 tablespoon expeller-pressed vegetable oil
1 small red onion, cut in half and thinly sliced lengthwise
1 small head of red cabbage, cored and sliced (5 to 6 cups)
1 tablespoon turbinado sugar
1¼ teaspoons kosher salt
½ cup cider vinegar
¼ cup red wine vinegar

Heat a large sauté pan over medium heat, and add the oil and onion. Sauté for 2 to 3 minutes, until softened and fragrant. Add the cabbage, sugar, and salt, and toss and cook for 2 minutes. Add the vinegars, toss again, and lower the heat. Cover and cook, stirring occasionally, for about 20 minutes—adding a little water as needed to keep it moist but not brothy—until tender. The cabbage will go from its raw purple to lavender to bright violet as it softens.

whole roasted onions

Preheat the oven to 425°F. Roast whole, unpeeled onions on a baking sheet for an hour or longer, until the skins are deep golden brown and blistered and the flesh is very tender throughout when pierced with a sharp knife. To serve, make a slit across the top of each onion with a sharp knife and insert a big pat of butter or spoonful of crème fraîche (see page 224). Serve with salt at the table.

THE BEE'S KNEES

I got a jewel of a gift in the mail today: six jars of single-variety honey from Italy. The chestnut honey is intense and stinky, possibly a taste that can only be acquired by living in a small Umbrian village; the kids scream when I make them smell it. Other flavors, like the rhododendron, the one cryptically labeled "forest," are hypnotic.

Honey is hot. Bees are the new backyard chickens, with hives sprouting up on urban rooftops and in suburban backyards while restaurateurs earnestly describe their "honey programs." When a request for tea brings you a special honey menu, a reasonable response might be "This whole honey thing has gone too far." But different honeys can offer an opportunity to visit another season and a place, translating the predominant fruit and flower that was feeding a hive of bees the moment their honey was made. During a flowering, bees tend not to merely immerse themselves in the same variety of nectar for weeks at a time but actually in the very same flower blossom.

Honey's popularity coincides with a dire moment for honeybees. The mysterious phenomenon that is now called "colony collapse disorder" was first noticed in late 2006, when bees began disappearing. Between then and early 2008—just a year and a half— approximately one third of adult worker bees had vanished, and they continue to at an alarming rate. Many of the likely contributors to CCD—exposure to high levels of pesticides and herbicides, viruses, parasites, overcrowding, loss of habitat, and a high level of stress, including poor nutrition—are the direct result of the industrial way in which honeybees are used in food production, which includes pollinating the plants that contribute to one third of our diet.

Rob Bowers and his wife, Cheri Whitted, keep bees to pollinate their biodynamic orchard and fruit crops on their Whitted Bowers Farm, near Hillsborough, north of Chapel Hill. Rob explains that honeys are often regionally specific. While bland clover honey is common in the North, not so in the South since clover blooms at the same time as the more delectable tulip poplar, which bees are mad for. According to our neighbor Scotty McLean (beekeeper, kimchi maker, and barbecue performance artist), 2007 was the best year ever. Other classic North Carolina honeys include sourwood, blueberry, black locust, and wild blackberry.

Rob and Cheri's melon blossom honey is my favorite, transmitting the complex flavors of the two acres of heirloom melons they plant every year. I fell in love before I understood the implications: As a rule, Whitted Bowers doesn't extract, or harvest, honey at all. Their bees are valued farmhands, and the most important use of their honey is as vital sustenance to get them through winter. Commercial honey producers generally replace the honey that they extract from their hives with sugar water; Rob and Cheri share in the honey only when they know that there is more than enough for the bees to stay healthy until spring. Of course, what is impossible to have is hopelessly irresistible, but in this case the very factors that prevent it from being available all the time are also exactly what make it worth waiting for.

honey frozen custard
with honeycomb candy

Alone, I am happy to eat butter cookies dipped in honey for dessert. This recipe is not quite as fast but is worth the time. It has the texture of perfect soft-serve ice cream, and since it's not actually a proper custard, no cooking is required.

SERVES 8

1½ cups heavy cream
4 large eggs, separated
Pinch of kosher salt
½ cup dark, flavorful honey, plus more for serving
Honeycomb Candy (recipe follows), for serving

In a medium bowl, whip the cream to soft peaks. Set aside.

In another medium bowl, beat the egg yolks, salt, and honey with an electric hand mixer until thickened, light yellow in color, and doubled in volume. In a third medium bowl, whip the egg whites to soft peaks. Fold the whipped cream into the yolk mixture, and then fold in the whites. Spoon into a 9 × 5-inch loaf pan and freeze until firm, at least 4 hours and up to several days.

To serve, spoon it out of the pan directly onto plates and serve with honeycomb shards.

honeycomb candy

MAKES ABOUT 6 CUPS OF SHARDS

¾ cup sugar
2 tablespoons honey
1½ teaspoons baking soda, sifted twice

Have ready a candy thermometer and a greased baking sheet.

Pour 2 tablespoons water into a deep medium saucepan. Add the sugar, and then drizzle the honey evenly over the top without stirring. Heat over medium-high heat until the

RECIPE CONTINUES

mixture reaches 300°F and is amber colored; do not let it go higher than 310°F. Remove from the heat, sprinkle with the baking soda, and using a small whisk, quickly combine in just four or five strokes, no more. Immediately pour the mixture onto the baking sheet and let it cool for about 20 minutes.

Break into shards and store in an airtight container for up to several days.

FAMILY MEAL

We don't have a scheduled staff meal or way of sitting down to eat at Lantern. Almost every day we eat lunch together, but it is often very fast and simple—an improvised shrimp cocktail with an experimental hot sauce, a salad, or a thrown-together soup. On especially crazy days, we don't eat at all except for bites here and there. If someone stops to think about it, we'll order in homemade pastrami, sauerkraut, and pickles from Neal's Deli, owned by Matt Neal and his wife, Sheila, who managed the Carrboro farmers' market before she and Matt opened a busy New York–style deli while raising kids on the side.

On special occasions we cook: for birthdays, maybe a big grilled steak; on a waiter's last night, something tasty but shocking like sauerbraten or an insane lasagna; in the case of an unusual hangover, Silvia can be persuaded to make Hangtown Fry—fresh oysters dipped in cracker crumbs, crisped in bacon fat, and tossed with lightly scrambled eggs and bacon. When we plan ahead, we really feast, and the fare tends to be Mexican, since that is where almost everyone in the kitchen grew up. During his five years as Lantern's dumpling master, Rudy Rodriguez made elaborate lunches, like moles that required starter kits carried from home on foot. His chilaquile period was legendary and immobilizing: freshly fried corn tortillas scrambled with eggs and spicy salsa until the eggs were creamy and the tortillas tender but still nicely chewy. We ate them three times a week for months until we all had to buy new pants. At a going-away party for Ramiro Vasquez, who was heading home to Mexico for the first time in eight years for his daughter's wedding, Dolores Vargas made delicate quesadillas with homemade wrappers so delicious that we now tease Ramiro (back in the States for another tour) that another meal of them might be worth losing him again.

Miguel Torres runs the kitchen at Lantern—by day he is in the kitchen cooking, tasting, and teaching, and he's there nearly every night, too, managing the details and chaos of service. For his thirtieth birthday, we made an epic ceviche of fat scallops, shrimp, and blue crab served with freshly fried tostadas; nearly fifty pounds were needed to counteract the beer and fuel the dancing. When Miguel moved here from his hometown, Celaya, near Mexico City, he was eighteen years old, had spoken English mainly in school, and knew only one person. One hundred friends showed up at the party—his "double quinceañera" to fond coworkers—and as usual he made sure that no one left hungry or "underserved."

As for staff meals, I think that we all would agree that the most critically acclaimed (and rarest) at Lantern are those that are completely homemade and don't involve eggs. With Valentine's weekend behind us, Miguel came in early today to make carnitas.

miguel torres's carnitas

On the few nights that he is not at Lantern, Miguel cooks Mexican at home. He has not seen his family since moving to North Carolina in 1999, and the goal of his home cooking is to make his dishes taste as close to his mother's and grandmother's as possible with the ingredients he can get here. He thinks that he is getting close with these carnitas.

SERVES 12, WITH LEFTOVERS

8 pounds boneless pork shoulder

2 cups lard

3 tablespoons kosher salt

½ teaspoon freshly ground black pepper

4 dried bay leaves

1 cup whole milk

1 cup Coca-Cola

1 orange, cut in half

Jalapeño and Red Onion Escabèche (recipe follows)

Green Cabbage Salad (recipe follows)

Salsa Verde and/or Salsa Roja (page 239)

Warm corn tortillas, for serving

Cut the pork shoulder into 3-inch cubes, trimming off any gristle as you go but leaving all the fat. Put the pork and the lard in a large, heavy pot over high heat. As soon as the lard has melted, add just enough cold water to barely cover the pork. Return to a boil and then reduce the heat to medium. Add the salt, pepper, and bay leaves, and stirring regularly, simmer briskly for about 1 hour, until the water has evaporated and the pork is nearly tender.

Raise the heat to medium-high and add the milk. Simmer for 5 minutes until the milk is almost completely reduced. Pour in the cola. Squeeze the orange halves over the meat and add the oranges to the pot, too. Cook for 10 to 15 minutes, stirring often, until the meat is crispy and deep caramel brown. Remove the orange halves and adjust the seasoning. Spoon the carnitas and some escabèche, cabbage salad, and salsa into each tortilla.

jalapeño and red onion escabeche

MAKES 3 CUPS

10 jalapeños, halved, seeded if desired, and thinly sliced lengthwise
4 medium red onions, thinly sliced
½ cup Escabeche Dressing (page 240)

In a medium bowl, combine the jalapeños and red onions with the dressing. Let sit at room temperature for at least 10 minutes and up to 2 hours before serving.

green cabbage salad

MAKES 4 CUPS

1 small head (about 1 pound) of green cabbage
2 medium carrots
1 bunch of radishes
½ cup Escabeche Dressing (page 240)

Remove and discard the outer layers of the cabbage. Cut the head in quarters, remove the core, and thinly slice the cabbage crosswise. Peel the carrots and slice them ¼ inch thick on the diagonal. Cut the slices into matchsticks. Slice the radishes into thin rounds. Combine the vegetables with the dressing and let sit at room temperature for at least 10 minutes and up to 2 hours before serving.

salsa verde

MAKES ABOUT 2 CUPS

1 (11-ounce) can tomatillos, drained
1 jalapeño, stemmed and cut into thick slices
¼ medium yellow onion, cut into 1-inch chunks
1 garlic clove
½ bunch fresh cilantro, thick stems cut off
½ teaspoon kosher salt

Put the tomatillos, jalapeño, onion, garlic, cilantro, and salt in a blender and process until smooth.

salsa roja

MAKES ABOUT 2 CUPS

6 ounces (about 7) dried guajillo chiles
1½ ounces (about 5) dried chiles, such as de Arbol
1 garlic clove
1 (11-ounce) can tomatillos
¼ medium yellow onion, finely diced
1 bunch fresh cilantro, thick stems cut off, leaves chopped
2½ teaspoons kosher salt

Stem and seed the chiles, and soak them in a bowl of hot water for 30 minutes. Drain, reserving ¾ cup of the liquid. Put the chiles, reserved soaking liquid, garlic, and tomatillos in a blender and process until smooth. Pour into a serving bowl and stir in the onion, cilantro, and salt.

escabeche dressing

MAKES 1 CUP

½ cup fresh lime juice
¼ cup plus 2 tablespoons distilled white vinegar
1 tablespoon plus 1 teaspoon kosher salt
1 teaspoon sugar
2 tablespoons extra virgin olive oil

Stir together the lime juice, vinegar, salt, and sugar in a small bowl until the salt and sugar dissolve. Whisk in the oil.

HOMELY VEGETABLES

I'm back from a dark, wet market earlier than usual and getting started on lunch. Big rough-skinned turnips, sweetly spicy, are going into a pot with onions and a small branch of rosemary to cook slowly for a warming late-morning soup.

Around this time every year, a suspicion creeps in at farmers' markets that there is nothing left to eat. This morning when I picked up one of Stanley Hughes's huge purple turnips, another shopper looked at me and laughed, "Never thought to eat a turnip." She graciously listened to the unsolicited recipe that followed but, fearing a lunch invitation, ran. Turnips are one of those vegetables that tend to hang around until the end of the market, sometimes making the trip back to the farm to become supper for the pigs. Even cold, hungry shoppers can't seem to make the leap to seeing them as food.

You could sell more turnips from a pot of soup than off a market table. Like cabbages and brawny rutabagas, they have a magical stone-soup feeling about them (you made this from that?), and the cold months are the best time to eat them. Many of these vegetables need long cooking to unlock their flavor—thorny, gnarled carrots and buttery yellow potatoes stewed together to make a soup with duck and cracklings; dense green cabbage salted for fortifying sauerkraut; beets simmered with aromatic spices and spiked with vinegar; or chunks of rutabaga simmered in a little water with a bit of salt and sugar and then coarsely mashed with butter. Others are fast—small, mild Japanese-style turnips roasted whole with honey or thinly sliced and gratinéed with cream; tender Savoy cabbage quickly braised with smoked ham or served just warmed in a slaw with caraway or in a raw winter crudité of black radishes; celery hearts and pale orange rutabaga with a warm fondue of Swiss cheese.

Until recently, most markets here in North Carolina shut down at the end of the fall, not to reopen until spring. But now that the demand for local food is starting to balance the risks that come with another growing season, more farmers are beginning to press on into the winter. At the Carrboro market in February, for instance, Michael and Jennifer Brinkley's stand is one of the most abundant. It's stacked with beets, fennel, cauliflower, early sping onions, curly red and flat black kale, purple mustard greens, several varieties of sweet potatoes including deep orange Beauregards and creamy white-fleshed O'Henrys, pork sausages, chickens, and nutty wheat flour and golden cornmeal, both grown and milled on the farm. And although farmers are certainly fewer at the winter market, so are shoppers. It's a kinder pace; no one is stepping on your foot to get the first asparagus and you have plenty of room to think about what to make for dinner.

turnip soup
with rosemary and black pepper

Carolina Gold rice "grits" from Anson Mills are short, uneven pieces of rice that have been broken during the threshing process. They cook up creamier than long-grain white rice, which can be substituted in this recipe: pulse it in batches in a spice mill or clean coffee grinder for 5 seconds to create the same effect.

SERVES 4 TO 6

1 small onion, minced
2 garlic cloves, minced
3 tablespoons olive oil
Kosher salt
½ cup dry white wine
6 cups chicken stock, preferably homemade (page 177), or water
½ cup Carolina Gold rice grits (see Sources, page 264)
Freshly ground black pepper
3 to 4 medium turnips, cut into ½-inch cubes
2 small branches fresh rosemary
3 tablespoons grated Parmesan cheese, or to taste

In a heavy 8-quart pot, sauté the onion and garlic in the olive oil over medium heat until tender and turning golden, about 5 minutes. Season with salt and pour in the wine and stock. Bring to a simmer and then add the rice grits, seasoning with salt and a little pepper. Simmer for 10 minutes, adjusting the heat as necessary. Then add the turnips and one of the rosemary branches. Continue to cook for about 15 minutes, stirring occasionally, until the turnips and rice are tender throughout.

While the soup cooks, pull the leaves off the remaining rosemary branches and roughly chop them.

Check the soup for seasoning and add more salt if needed. Discard the rosemary branch. Spoon the soup into bowls, and garnish with a generous grinding of black pepper, some chopped rosemary leaves, and the Parmesan.

sautéed savoy cabbage
with speck and lemon

Speck is a cured Austrian ham, similar to prosciutto except that it is lightly spiced and smoked. Prosciutto or thinly sliced uncooked bacon may be substituted. (If using bacon, cook until nearly rendered, 3 minutes.)

SERVES 4 AS A SIDE DISH

1 large head of Savoy cabbage (about 1 pound)
1 tablespoon olive oil
2 garlic cloves, cut lengthwise into thirds
4 thin slices of speck, any rind removed, torn into rough pieces
½ teaspoon kosher salt
1 cup chicken stock, preferably homemade (page 177)
Juice of 1 lemon

Discard any bruised outer leaves from the cabbage. Remove the leaves from the core and tear them into rough pieces, discarding the tough central stems.

Heat the oil in a large sauté pan over medium heat. Add the garlic and sauté until it just starts to color, about 2 minutes. Add the speck and stir to coat it in the oil. Add the cabbage, season with the salt, toss to combine, and add the stock. Simmer until the cabbage leaves are just tender, about 4 minutes. Stir in the lemon juice just before serving.

roasted japanese turnips with honey

These small turnips are typically sold with their tender green leaves attached, and those can be braised like any other winter green (see page 219).

SERVES 4

4 bunches (about 20 small) golf-ball-size Japanese-style turnips,
    stems trimmed to ¼ inch, sliced in half lengthwise
1 tablespoon plus 1 teaspoon expeller-pressed vegetable oil
½ teaspoon kosher salt
Freshly ground black pepper
1 tablespoon honey
Pinch of cayenne

In a medium bowl, toss the turnips with 1 tablespoon oil, the salt, and some pepper.

Heat a large cast-iron pan over medium-high heat. When it is quite hot, coat the pan with the remaining 1 teaspoon oil and add the turnips. Reduce the heat to medium and toss the turnips. Sauté, shaking the pan frequently, until the turnips are starting to turn golden brown, especially on the cut sides, and are almost tender but still slightly firm, 8 to 10 minutes.

In a small bowl, combine the honey and cayenne with 1 tablespoon water. Add this to the turnips and cook, tossing for another few minutes, until the turnips are tender.

choucroute garnie 1-2-3

Choucroute garnie traditionally combines sausages and thick chunks of bacon with larger cuts of meat like smoked pork chops and even hunks of pork shoulder. This faster version includes only sausages and bacon. The grated potato adds body and silkiness to the sauerkraut, which, if not homemade (see page 143), should be purchased refrigerated (not canned).

SERVES 8

2 tablespoons duck fat, lard, or expeller-pressed vegetable oil

2 medium onions, diced

2 cups grated peeled russet potato (about 1 large potato)

Kosher salt

2½ pounds drained sauerkraut (12 cups loosely packed homemade [page 143] or
    1 [32-ounce] jar or equivalent, drained and lightly rinsed)

2 dried bay leaves

10 dried juniper berries, lightly crushed

5 black peppercorns

1½ cups dry white wine

2 to 3 cups chicken stock, preferably homemade (page 177), or water, as needed

1-pound chunk of unsliced slab bacon, cut into several large chunks

2 pounds mixed pork sausages, such as knockwurst, boudin blanc, and/or fresh garlic
    sausages

Mustard, for serving

Preheat the oven to 350°F.

Heat the fat in a heavy, shallow 3-quart enameled cast-iron pot or other heatproof baking dish over low heat. Sauté the onions until soft and fragrant but not browned, about 8 minutes. Stir in the potatoes, season lightly with salt, and cook until wilted, 2 to 3 minutes. Add the sauerkraut, bay leaves, juniper berries, peppercorns, wine, and just enough stock to nearly cover the sauerkraut. Bring to a simmer and remove from the heat.

Nestle the bacon into the sauerkraut, cover, and bake in the oven for 30 minutes, until the bacon is starting to render. Remove the cover and add the sausages in one layer, pushing them down a bit into the sauerkraut, which should still be quite moist. If it seems dry, moisten it with a little additional chicken stock. Bake, uncovered, for 45 minutes to 1 hour, until the top of the sauerkraut is golden and the sausages and bacon are cooked through and browned. Bring the dish to the table and serve with strong mustard and lots of cold beer or white wine.

curried beets

SERVES 6 TO 8 GENEROUSLY AS AN APPETIZER

¼ cup expeller-pressed vegetable oil
1 medium yellow onion, finely diced
½ cup finely julienned fresh ginger
2 tablespoons garam masala
1 dried red chile, such as de Arbol
3 pounds small beets, 2 to 3 inches in diameter, stems trimmed, peeled,
    and quartered lengthwise
2 tablespoons kosher salt
½ cup distilled white vinegar
Crème fraîche (page 224) and nigella seeds (sometimes mislabeled black onion seeds),
    for serving, optional

Heat the oil in a large heavy pot over medium heat. Add the onion, reduce the heat to low, and cover. Cook for 10 to 12 minutes, stirring occasionally, until the onion is translucent and soft but has not colored. Add the ginger, garam masala, and chile. Raise the heat to high and toast the spices for about 1 minute, stirring the whole time. Add the beets, 5 cups water, and the salt, and bring to a boil. Reduce the heat and simmer for 15 to 20 minutes, until the beets are just tender. Remove from the heat and add the vinegar. Adjust the seasoning and remove the chile.

Serve in warm bowls as is or garnished with a spoonful of crème fraiche and sprinkled with nigella seeds.

OVERNIGHT COOKING

The first time, it was practically an accident. Stuck out at our old house outside of town on a freezing night with houseguests, a power outage, and a whole duck in the fridge, it occurred to me that I could solve two problems at once. We stayed up late by the fireplace and put the duck in the (propane-fueled) oven at 200°F before going to bed around 3 a.m. The cooking smells pulled us from our beds into the toasty kitchen for coffee in the morning and the duck became a satisfying lazy lunch with mashed rutabagas to soak up the juices (just chunks of rutabagas simmered until tender in water seasoned with salt and a little sugar, then mashed with soft butter). A far cry from a rare, seared nouvelle-cuisine breast, this was a duck of the old school, with completely tender meat and crisp, burnished skin.

Super-slow cooking (whether during the day or, if you stay up late and rise early, overnight) extends the rewards of work in the kitchen—the delicious smell and the cozy feeling—without adding any extra time or effort. And actual cooking aside, I love anything that makes itself: yogurt placed in a warm spot on the stove; a cool, slow rise for no-knead bread or pizza dough; or an eggy Dutch pancake batter made in minutes with an immersion blender and then left in the refrigerator until morning. Even something as simple as soaking beans overnight gives me a sense of accomplishment.

But these overnight projects are more than just fun: soaked beans cook rapidly and have a velvety texture; a Dutch pancake made from batter that has rested is so fluffy, it rises out of the skillet; and the bread has an amazing airy crumb. Overnight beef short ribs are tender enough to eat with a spoon and their broth is clean, clear, and intense. Super-slow brisket has the time to build real flavor along with the sweet caramelized onions that, by morning, have become gravy. It's a good trick to stumble into the kitchen in the morning and open the oven door to a complete meal—as if you were on a cooking show. But, if you are like me, what grabs you is the comfort to the animal brain of knowing where your next meal is coming from.

overnight pot-on-fire

SERVES 4 TO 6

4 pounds bone-in beef short ribs
1 tablespoon plus 1 teaspoon kosher salt
1 teaspoon freshly ground black pepper
2 tablespoons expeller-pressed vegetable oil
1 cup (about 1 ounce) dried porcini mushrooms
1 large yellow onion, cut into quarters
1 head of garlic, unpeeled, cut in half crosswise
1 bunch (about 12 medium) radishes
2 medium carrots, or 1 bunch baby carrots
1 bunch spring onions, or 1 medium leek
Horseradish, mustard, coarse sea salt, and pickles, for serving

Trim the silverskin and any excess fat off the short ribs, and season them with the
1 tablespoon salt and the pepper. Refrigerate for at least 6 hours or overnight.

Preheat the oven to 225°F.

Heat a heavy pot or Dutch oven over medium-high heat, and add the oil. Sear the ribs
on all sides until deep golden brown, about 10 minutes. Remove the meat and discard any
remaining oil. Put the ribs back in the pot, meat side down. Add enough cold water to cover
the ribs by 2 inches (about 3 quarts). Bring the liquid to a simmer and cook, repeatedly
skimming off any foam, for 10 to 15 minutes. Add the porcini, onion, garlic, and remaining
1 teaspoon salt. Bring back to a simmer. Tent the meat with a piece of parchment or
aluminum foil by placing it on top and then crimping it snugly around the ribs so that the
edges nearly meet the liquid. Cover the pot with a tight-fitting lid, transfer it to the oven,
and braise for 6 hours.

Trim the radishes, leaving about ¾ inch of green stem. Unless they are very small, cut
them in half. Cut the carrots on the diagonal into ½-inch-thick rounds; or, if using baby
carrots, peel and trim them, leaving ¾ inch of the green stem. Trim the spring onions or
leek and slice into chunks (wash the leek well). One vegetable at a time, blanch in boiling
salted water until just tender.

Remove the ribs and strain the broth through a fine-mesh sieve into a saucepan. Skim
the fat from the broth; then add the blanched vegetables to the broth and reheat gently.
Adjust seasoning and serve the ribs and vegetables in the broth with the accompaniments.

onion-braised overnight brisket

SERVES 8 TO 10

1 (4-pound) beef brisket, trimmed
4 teaspoons kosher salt
1 teaspoon freshly ground black pepper, or to taste
1 large garlic clove
4 tablespoons expeller-pressed vegetable oil
4 large yellow onions, thinly sliced
1 teaspoon sugar

Season the fatty side of the brisket with 1 teaspoon of the salt and ½ teaspoon of the pepper. Flip the brisket over.

On a cutting board, chop the garlic. Add 1 teaspoon of the salt while continuing to chop, stopping occasionally to mash the garlic to a paste by holding your knife almost flat against the board with the dull side facing you and sliding it across the garlic to crush it. Rub the garlic paste into the non-fatty side of the brisket and season it with the remaining ½ teaspoon pepper. Starting with the thin side, roll the brisket up tight, jelly-roll style, with the fat on the outside, and tie it firmly with kitchen twine.

Heat a Dutch oven or other heavy pot over medium-high heat and add 1 tablespoon of the oil. Brown the brisket evenly on all sides, about 20 minutes, and then transfer it to a platter.

Meanwhile, preheat the oven to 225°F.

Discard any remaining oil in the pot, wipe it out with a paper towel, and return the pot to the stove over medium-low heat. Add the remaining 3 tablespoons oil, the onions, the sugar, and the remaining 2 teaspoons salt. Cook, stirring often, for 15 to 20 minutes, until the onions are completely soft and caramelized.

Remove the pot from the heat and add 1 cup water. Return the brisket to the pot, and use a slotted spoon to spread some of the onions on top to keep it moist. Tent it with a piece of parchment or aluminum foil by placing it on top and then crimping it snugly around the roast so that the edges nearly meet the liquid, and then cover the pot with a tight-fitting lid. Put the pot in the oven and braise for 7 hours, until the brisket is tender.

Transfer the brisket to a warm place and use a food mill to puree the onions. Return the onion puree to the pot and heat gently, adding a little water if necessary to make a thick but pourable gravy. Slice the brisket and serve with the onion gravy.

COOK IT WHOLE

This afternoon at work, I made a terrine from a pig's head and some chunky feet for extra oomph. A few hours in the pot with warm spices like star anise and cassia, heady fish sauce, and white wine, and the meat is delicately flavored and silky enough to be thinly sliced, spiced up with aromatic Vietnamese black pepper, and served with warm buttered bread and pickled turnips. Waiters used to dread explaining "head-to-tail" dishes to customers, but in these pig-obsessed times, they sell well along with barbecued tails and ear salad. The revival of whole-animal cooking was fueled by chefs on the prowl for "new" food and deeper flavors but also in support of the farms they love. Selling each and every part of an animal, from cheeks to shanks to skin, helps farms move towards break-even, and having a market for "the odd bits" has been an essential part of the rise in small-scale livestock production. Piedmont North Carolina farmers now have waitlists for pork belly, chicken feet, and schmaltz.

But a rabbit has only two kidneys and each ox a single tail, and as tasty as they are deep-fried, no farmer is going make it selling cockscombs. What they do need to sell more of is happily mundane and feasible: whole chickens! Because of high processing costs, it's impossible for farms to thrive selling boneless breasts, so simply finding a group of steady customers willing to buy whole birds is more useful than an entire kick line of offal-loving chefs.

If you usually cook chicken parts or boneless meat, dealing with a whole bird may seem like a lot of work, but it's not. A small chicken can be prepped for the oven in just a few minutes and cooked in about forty-five. Aside from simple roasting, my everyday way of handling a whole chicken efficiently is the Chinese "no poach" method, which delivers a tender pile of perfectly cooked meat and a bowlful of broth with minimum effort.

roast chicken with fennel and spring onions

Cooking and cleaning pigs' heads all day gave me a powerful hunger for chicken. This is an especially aromatic roasted chicken with an all-in-one sauce and side dish.

SERVES 4

1 (3½- to 4-pound) chicken
4 tablespoons (½ stick) unsalted butter, at room temperature
Kosher salt and freshly ground black pepper
2 teaspoons expeller-pressed vegetable oil
2 fennel bulbs, preferably with green fronds
8 bulbing spring onions with green tops
6 garlic cloves, smashed and peeled
½ cup dry white wine
½ cup chicken stock, preferably homemade (page 177; or see Note)

Allow the chicken to come to room temperature, up to 1 hour.

Preheat the oven to 425°F.

Rinse the chicken under cold running water and pat it dry. Remove the wing tips, reserving them with the neck for broth if desired (see Note). Coat the chicken with 1 tablespoon of the butter, and season it inside and out with a generous amount of salt and pepper.

Coat a large, heavy roasting pan with 1 teaspoon of the oil. Trim the fennel and spring onion bulbs, reserving the fennel fronds and green onion tops. Cut each fennel bulb and the onions in half lengthwise and then into ½-inch-wide lengthwise slices. In a medium bowl, toss the fennel, onion bulbs, and garlic with ¼ teaspoon salt and the remaining 1 teaspoon oil to coat. Arrange the vegetables in the roasting pan, put the chicken on top, and roast in the oven for 30 minutes.

In the meantime, slice the green onion tops into thin rings, and tear the fennel fronds into small sprigs to make about 3 cups total.

Reduce the oven temperature to 375°F and give the vegetables a stir so that they color evenly. Roast for another 20 to 25 minutes, until the chicken is done—the skin will be crisp and deep golden brown, the juices will have just a tinge of light pink, and an instant-read thermometer placed in the thickest part of the thigh will read 165°F.

Remove the pan from the oven. Transfer the chicken to a platter, tent it with foil, and let it rest for 10 minutes. In the meantime, if the fennel and onions are not yet golden brown, return them to the oven to roast for another few minutes on their own until they are well caramelized.

Put the roasting pan over medium-high heat and add the wine and stock, scraping the bottom of the pan and stirring the vegetables. Simmer for about 3 minutes, until the sauce has a slightly syrupy consistency. Add the fennel fronds and green onion tops. Remove the pan from the heat and add the remaining 3 tablespoons butter, swirling it in until it dissolves and thickens the sauce.

Carve the chicken into serving pieces, adding any juices that accumulate on the carving board to the sauce. With a slotted spoon, spread the vegetables on a warm serving platter. Arrange the chicken over the vegetables, and spoon the sauce on top.

Note: It's simple to make a light chicken broth by simmering the neck and wing tips in cold water with some aromatics like a slice or two of carrot and onion, a garlic clove, and a few peppercorns for about 45 minutes, about the time the chicken is in the oven.

no-poach poached chicken

Rinse a 3- to 4-pound bird well and rub it all over with a generous amount of kosher salt. Place the bird and its neck in a pot that fits them comfortably. Fill the pot with cold water to cover by about an inch, and add aromatics: garlic, fresh ginger, scallions, and sherry; or dried chiles, cumin seeds, and bay leaves; or wine, fresh thyme, leeks, and black peppercorns. Bring to a boil over high heat, and then immediately reduce the heat so the water simmers. Check the seasoning of the stock; it should be as salty as a well-seasoned soup broth. Simmer for 5 minutes and then remove from the heat. Cover tightly and let sit for about 1 hour. The chicken will be perfectly cooked: the white meat still juicy and rosy at the bone, and the dark just done as well. Let the chicken cool completely in the broth. Remove the bird, leaving the liquid and aromatics behind in the pot.

With a little more time, you can make a more flavorful stock: Pick the meat from the bones, and reserving the meat, return the bones to the pot. Bring the broth to a simmer, add additional flavorings if desired, and cook for 1 hour or longer, adding water as necessary. With lots of chicken and a rich stock, you have an on-the-spot chicken soup; you can make a cold chicken salad from the pulled breast meat and a little of the broth seasoned with lemon, roasted walnut oil, and scallions; or you can stew the dark meat further in the broth with ground chiles and hominy.

roasted spareribs with crushed fennel and red chiles

SERVES 4 TO 6

2 racks (about 5 pounds) pork spareribs
2 tablespoons expeller-pressed vegetable oil
2 small dried red chiles, such as de Arbol
1 tablespoon fennel seeds
Kosher salt and freshly ground black pepper

Preheat the oven to 450°F.

Drizzle the ribs with the oil and rub it in evenly. In a clean spice or coffee grinder, pulse the chiles and fennel seeds until coarsely but fairly evenly ground. Season the ribs on both sides with the mixture, and with a generous amount of salt and pepper. Put the ribs on a rack in a roasting pan and roast for 15 minutes.

Reduce the oven temperature to 375°F and roast, rotating the pan halfway through cooking, for 1 to 1¼ hours, until the meat is tender and deep golden brown, and easily pulls away from the bones.

WATERCRESS FROM A STREAM

For about six weeks at the end of winter and the very beginning of spring, the cold stream that runs through a small wooded valley on Daniel Tolfree's Millarckee Farm fills with watercress. His farm is just twenty-three acres—standing at one end of his land you could almost hear his distinctive, easy laugh from the other—but it has the environmental diversity you might see within five hundred acres. The earth is veined with soapstone and quartz and small springs; the fields where he grows his spicy greens and herbs make up only a few acres and are surrounded by meadows of grasses filled with beneficial insects and stands of first-growth hardwoods and pine forests. The soil is gorgeous and loamy, rich with thousands of years of silt from Cane Creek, which winds through the land and floods his lower fields during big storms every five or ten years.

The stream where his watercress grows is its own narrow microclimate, much cooler than the rest of the farm. Harvesting watercress, he can spend hours in the middle of the stream—usually barefoot as it warms up—as he picks each stem by hand. The watercress starts off very small and tender and grows more peppery each week until it begins to flower, tiny bright white blooms on deep green—and then it's gone.

Watercress, an ancient vegetable, is also a world-wide plant. Daniel has customers who recognize it from childhoods lived in Laos, Bolivia, and the Himalayas. In general he won't sell it to us at the restaurant, preferring to keep it for his loyal market regulars, to whom he enjoys selling more than to fickle chefs. He has been hard to get in touch with for the last few days and so I am up early, thinking that this is the week.

Farm-driven cooking using ingredients that taste like themselves is the goal of a great many chefs, and it makes sense: even at the most rarified restaurant, the highest compliment we give the food is that a pea foam actually tastes like a sweet pea, or that a peach dessert tastes like a real, ripe peach. But it is a bit of a myth that chefs always have the greatest access to the best ingredients: with the exception of hard-to-find exotic things, like dry-aged prime beef or fresh wasabi, a home cook who is in touch with local farmers often has greater access to better ingredients than restaurant chefs do. At home, a quart of the sweetest strawberries or just-picked peas, or a dozen eggs from chickens that spent most of their time in the woods, will start a good many meals. In a restaurant, where the volume is greater and consistency is required, ingredients purchased by the flat often can't live up, even when they can actually be ordered in quantity.

Watercress from very pure water like the stream at Millarckee Farm is a once-a-year treat, and its juicy leaves and crunchy stems are more succulent and spicy than what you find any other time. It won't be for sale in any restaurant tonight, but everyone who makes it to the Millarckee Farm stand before 9:00 this morning will have a few bunches.

watercress with a fried egg and black sesame sauce

SERVES 4

1½ teaspoons fresh lime juice
Kosher salt
1½ tablespoons expeller-pressed vegetable oil, plus more for frying the eggs
2 bunches of watercress, tough stems trimmed
4 large eggs
¼ cup Black Sesame Sauce (recipe follows), or more to taste

In a medium bowl, mix together the lime juice, a big pinch of salt, and the oil with a fork or a whisk. Add the watercress and toss gently to lightly coat. Divide the dressed watercress among four salad plates and set aside.

Heat a cast-iron or other heavy skillet that you like to use for eggs over medium-high heat. When it is hot, swirl a small amount of vegetable oil in the pan and crack in the eggs, in batches if necessary. When the edges of the eggs are a bit crispy, the whites are completely set, and the yolks are still runny, transfer an egg to each plate so that it slightly overlaps the watercress. Season the eggs with salt, and drizzle about a tablespoon of the sesame sauce over each portion.

black sesame sauce

At Lantern, we use this sauce on vegetables like meaty steamed Roma beans, and also on thinly sliced raw beef along with homemade hot sauce and a tiny pile of dressed spicy greens.

MAKES ½ CUP

¼ cup black sesame seeds
½ teaspoon kosher salt
½ teaspoon expeller-pressed vegetable oil
1 tablespoon sake
1 tablespoon mirin
¼ cup Dashi (recipe follows), chicken stock, or water

Toast the sesame seeds in a small sauté pan over medium heat, tossing frequently, until the seeds become fragrant and begin to pop. Transfer them to a plate and let them cool completely. Grind in 10-second increments in a spice mill or clean coffee grinder to a very fine paste, stirring the mixture, then grinding again, and repeating this process until the paste is completely smooth and glistening from the oil that has been released. This will take 3 to 5 minutes. (If the seeds are not ground into a very smooth paste, the sauce will be gray rather than deep black.) Transfer the paste to a small bowl, add the salt, and gradually whisk in the oil, sake, mirin, and dashi until smooth.

dashi

Leftover dashi freezes well and can become a fast miso soup or used instead of water to poach vegetables or cook grains.

MAKES ABOUT 2½ CUPS

5 dried black mushrooms
1 (1 × 4-inch) strip of kombu
3 tablespoons bonito flakes

Put 3 cups water and the mushrooms in a nonreactive saucepan and bring to a simmer. Turn the heat to low, cover, and cook at a very gentle simmer for 10 minutes. Add the kombu and simmer very gently for 5 minutes. Remove from the heat and add the bonito flakes. Let steep, covered, for 8 minutes. Strain through a fine-mesh sieve. Discard the solids and use the broth as you would stock.

SOURCES

A&B Milling Company
North Carolina peanuts from Halifax
County.
www.auntrubyspeanuts.com

Adriana's Caravan
A wide variety of exotic pantry
ingredients including spices, canned
tomatillos, and verjus.
www.adrianascaravan.com

Animal Welfare Approved
Independent third-party certification
for humanely raised pasture and range-
based meat, dairy, and eggs.
www.animalwelfareapproved.com

The American Chestnut Foundation
The mission of TACF is to restore the
American chestnut to its native range.
Annual membership includes Restoration
chestnut seed stock, twenty-six years in
the making.
www.acf.org

American Livestock Breeds
Conservancy
The ALBC has worked since 1977 to
protect 150 breeds of livestock and
poultry from extinction.
www.albc-usa.org

Anson Mills
Carolina Gold rice, Sea Island peas,
and stone-ground, cold-milled heirloom
grains.
www.ansonmills.com

Caw Caw Creek Farm
Pasture-raised heritage pork, including
Ossabaw raised in Calhoun County,
South Carolina.
www.cawcawcreek.com

Center for Environmental Farming
Systems
CEFS develops farming and food
systems that protect the environment and
strengthen local communities.
www.cefs.ncsu.edu

Century Farm Orchards
Old southern apples and pear trees.
www.centuryfarmorchards.com

Chefs Collaborative
A national network of chefs working to
foster a more sustainable food system.
www.chefscollaborative.com

Despaña
High-quality olive oil–packed anchovies
and other Spanish ingredients.
www.despanabrandfoods.com

Eat Wild
Information on grass-fed animal
products and direct links to local farms.
www.eatwild.com

Eden Foods
Ume plum vinegar.
www.edenfoods.com

Edible Landscaping
Large selection of fruit and nut trees
and plants, including figs, native
persimmons, chestnuts, pawpaws, and
muscadine grapes.
www.ediblelandscaping.com

Field and Forest Products
Information about mushroom cultivation
and supplies.
www.fieldforest.net

Frontier Co-op
Organic and sustainably sourced spices
and herbs, including Anaheim chiles and
dried elderflowers.
www.frontiercoop.com

Good Shepherd Poultry Ranch
Frank Reese's pasture-raised heritage
chicken, turkey, duck, and geese.
www.goodshepherdpoultryranch.com

Heritage Foods USA
Pasture-raised pork, heritage turkey,
Piedmontese beef, goat, bison, rabbit,
charcuterie, and rare Native American
foods, from small producers.
www.heritagefoodsusa.com

Hudson Valley Foie Gras
Moulard duck and other duck products.
www.hudsonvalleyfoiegras.com

Kitazawa Seed
Asian vegetable seeds, including shishito
peppers and edamame.
www.kitazawaseed.com

The Lee Brothers Boiled Peanut
Catalogue
Southern specialties, including boiled
peanuts, pickles, preserves, and grains.
www.boiledpeanuts.com

L'Hoste Citrus
Organic citrus from a family farm in
Louisiana.
www.lhostecitrus.com

Local Harvest
Listings for farms, farmers' markets, and
CSAs by state and zip code.
www.localharvest.org

Monterey Bay Aquarium Seafood Watch
Guide to sustainable seafood choices.
www.montereybayaquarium.org

Muddy Pond Sorghum
Championship sorghum from the
Guenther family in Tennessee.
www.muddypondsorghum.com

Murray's
A vast selection of artisan cheese.
www.murrayscheese.com

Mutual Trading Company
High-quality Japanese ingredients,
including bonito, kombu, sansho, and
dried black mushrooms.
www.lamtc.com

New Hope Seed Company
Heirloom seeds and sweet potato starts.
www.newhopeseed.com

Pollinator Partnership
Regional planting guides to create
pollinator friendly habitats.
www.pollinator.org

Rancho Gordo
Heirloom beans, dried corn, chiles,
grains, and rice.
www.ranchogordo.com

Rutgers Extension
Ramapo tomato seeds.
www.njfarmfresh.rutgers.edu/
jerseytomato.html

S. Wallace Edwards & Sons, Inc.
Ham, bacon, and sausage since 1926,
now including a line from pasture-raised
Berkshire hogs.
www.edwardsvaham.com

Saxelby Cheesemongers
American farmstead cheese, mostly from
the northeast.
www.saxelbycheese.com

Seed Savers
Thirty-five-year-old nonprofit
organization dedicated to saving and
sharing heirloom seeds.
www.seedsavers.org

Seeds
South Eastern Efforts Developing
Sustainable Spaces, Inc.
www.seedsnc.org

Southern Exposure Seed Exchange
Heirloom seeds, including field peas.
www.southernexposure.com

Sunburst Trout Company
Farm-raised trout and caviar from the
Blue Ridge Mountains in Canton, North
Carolina.
www.sunbursttrout.com

Utz
Potato chips; the Grandma Utz Kettle
line is fried in lard.
www.utzsnacks.com/index.html

White Boot Brigade
Wild shrimp from Louisiana.
www.whitebootbrigade.org

White Mountain
Hand-crank and electric ice-cream-
makers.
www.whitemountainproducts.com

Zingerman's Mail Order
Traditionally made foods including
unusual artisan pantry ingredients,
breads, and handmade cheeses.
www.zingermans.com

Local Markets

Carrboro Farmers' Market
www.carrborofarmersmarket.com

Cliff's Meat Market
100 West Main Street
Carrboro, North Carolina

Durham Farmers' Market
www.durhamfarmersmarket.com

Johnnys
901 West Main Street
Carrboro, North Carolina
www.johnnyscarrboro.com

NC Farm Fresh
A listing of farmers markets in North
Carolina.
www.ncfarmfresh.com

Tom Robinson's Seafood
207 Roberson Street
Carrboro, North Carolina

Local Farms and Producers

Acre Station Meat Farm, Ronnie and
Richard Huettmann
Pinetown, North Carolina
www.acrestationmeatfarm.com

Ayrshire Farm, Bill Dow
Pittsboro, North Carolina

Braeburn Farm, Charles Sydner
Snow Camp, North Carolina
www.braeburnfarms.com

Brinkley Farms, Michael and Jennifer
Brinkley
Creedmoor, North Carolina
www.brinkleyfarms.com

Cane Creek Farm, Eliza McLean
Snow Camp, North Carolina
www.canecreekfarm.us

Castlemaine Farm, Joann and Brian
Gallagher
Liberty, North Carolina
www.castlemainefarm.blogspot.com

Catbriar Farm, Sara and Graham
Broadwell
Blanch, North Carolina

Chapel Hill Creamery, Flo Hawley and
Portia McKnight
Chapel Hill, North Carolina
www.southerncheese.com

Chicken Bridge Bakery, Rob and Monica
Segovia-Welsh
Pittsboro, North Carolina
www.chickenbridgebakery.weebly.com

Coon Rock Farm, Richard and Jamie
Holcomb
Hillsborough, North Carolina
www.coonrockfarm.com

Eco Farm, John and Cindy Soehner
Chapel Hill, North Carolina
www.ecofarmnc.com

Ferguson Farm, John Ferguson
Cameron, North Carolina

Fickle Creek Farm and Bed and
Breakfast, Ben Bergmann and Noah
Ranells
Efland, North Carolina
www.home.mebtel.net/~ficklecreek/

Foggy Ridge Cider, Diane Flynt
Dugspur, Virginia
www.foggyridgecider.com

Fowl Attitude Farm, Doug and Heidi
Brown
Cedar Grove, North Carolina

High Rock Farm, Richard Teague
Gibsonville, North Carolina

J+B Aquafood, Bonnie and Jim
Swartzenberg
Holly Ridge, North Carolina

Levering Orchard, Frank Levering
Ararat, Virginia
www.leveringorchard.com

Lil' Farm, George O'Neal
Timberlake, North Carolina
www.lilfarm.com

Millarckee Farm, Daniel Tolfree
Graham, North Carolina

Mountain Gardens, Joe Hollis
Burnsville, North Carolina
www.mountaingardensherbs.com

Peregrine Farm, Alex and Betsy Hitt
Graham, North Carolina
www.peregrinefarm.net

Perry-winkle Farm, Mike Perry and
Cathy Jones
Chapel Hill, North Carolina

Pine Knot Farm, Stanley Hughes
Hurdle Mills, North Carolina

Small Potatoes Farm, Simon Rose and
Natasha McCurley
Chapel Hill, North Carolina

Southern Heritage Apple Orchard at
Horne Creek Farm
Pinnacle, North Carolina
www.nchistoricsites.org

Sunburst Trout Farm, Sally and Steve
Eason
Canton, North Carolina
www.sunbursttrout.com

Whitted Bowers Farm, Rob Bowers and
Cheri Whitted
Cedar Grove, North Carolina
www.whittedbowersfarm.com

Local Restaurants

Lantern
423 West Franklin Street
Chapel Hill, North Carolina
www.lanternrestaurant.com

Neal's Deli
100 East Main Street
Carrboro, North Carolina
www.nealsdeli.com

Sanitary Fish Market and Restaurant,
501 Evans Street
Morehead City, North Carolina
www.sanitaryfishmarket.com

Scratch Baking
111 Orange Street
Durham, North Carolina
www.piefantasy.com

Toast
345 West Main Street
Durham, North Carolina
www.toast-fivepoints.com

ACKNOWLEDGMENTS

My thanks go to David Kuhn, for convincing me not only that I could write a book, but that it would also be fun; Rica Allannic, for her thoughtful and patient editing; Doris Cooper, Lauren Shakely, Marysarah Quinn, and Kate Tyler, for their support and enthusiasm for this project; John Kernick, for his strong vision and commitment; David Doernberg, for his frequent advice and solutions; Rebecca Blazak, for her smart shopping and propping; Silvia Pahola, for her friendship and essential input on everything from pig wrangling to recipe development; Jane Daniels Lear, for her critical early read and suggestions; Monica Segovia-Welsh, for her wisdom in the world of pastry and beyond; Miguel Torres, Jason Wall, and Lindsay Griffin, whose leadership and long hours at Lantern made a book a possibility; Phil Morrison, for his keen, repeated reading and ideas.

To the many the farmers, producers, and cooks who generously shared their knowledge and stories—Ben Bergmann and Noah Ranells, John and Cindy Soehner, Sara and Graham Broadwell, Frank Reese, Cliff Collins, Rob Bowers and Cheri Whitted, Cliff Collins, Flo Hawley and Portia McKnight, Lee and Edith Calhoun, William Rubel, Bill Dow and Daryl Walker, Billy Cotter, Peter Holzman and Diane Gillis, Scotty McLean, Matt and Sheila Neal, Phoebe Lawless, George O'Neal, Daniel Tolfree, Joe Hollis, Cathy Jones and Mike Perry, Alex and Betsy Hitt, David Auerbach, Diane Flynt, Charles Sydnor, Brandon and Andrea Williams, Eliza MacLean, Michael and Jennifer Brinkley, Richard Teague, Jim Swartzenberg, Frank Levering, Gabe Hart, Sam Suchoff, Stanley Hughes, Simon Rose and Natasha McCurley, Glenn Roberts, Helga and Tim MacAller, Stock, Linda and Lester L'Hoste, Rob Segovia-Welsh, Bernie Herman, Kay Hamrick, and Salvador Bonilla.

To the late Tom Robinson; he is missed here every day.

To many people in North Carolina working behind the scenes to help farms grow and thrive who offered ideas and information, including Nancy Creamer and John O'Sullivan of the Center for Environmental Farming Systems, revolutionary extension agent Debbie Roos, Emily Lancaster of Animal Welfare Approved, Sandi Kronick of Eastern Carolina Organics, Marjie Bender of the American Livestock Breeds Conservancy, Sarah Blacklin of the Carrboro Farmers Market, Kavanah Ramsier of SEEDS, Tandy Jones of the Triangle Land Conservancy, Scott Marlow of Rural Advancement Foundation International, and Fawn Pattison of Toxic Free North Carolina.

To friends and family who provided ideas and encouragement—Pat Coller, Kristen Beard, Fran McCullough, Jennifer Noble Kelly, Alan Stern, Jennifer Wilson, Sally Miller, Tracey Tomlinson and Lane Wurster, Jenne Scherer, Catlin Hettel, Christina Anglin, Tricia Mesigian, Reuben Ayres, Jamie Fiocco, Marilyn Markel, Kathy Hudson, Heather and Jason Ross, Tom Reardon, Katharine Walton, Mark Dauman, Tina Marrie, Maggie Fost, Nancie McDermott, Mollie Stevens, Ari Weinzweig, Kirsten Bachmann, Pat Boes, Kelly Alexander, Amelia Durand, Colin Dodd, Dorothy Allen, and Ralph and Sue McCaughan.

To my Lantern family, past and present, especially Ric Palao, Fernando Morales, Wesley and Jen Wolfe, Ramiro Vasquez, Charlotte Walton, Emily Rutter, Kristen Johnson, and John Korzekwinski.

To my brother Brendan, for his good humor and friendship before, during, and after we opened a restaurant; my brother Tim, for his constant counsel; my sister, Emily, for her inspiration; and my parents, Kathe and Vince, for their steady love and support.

And thanks with all my heart to Mac, Oona, and Arthur. I am so lucky to be at your table.

INDEX

Note: Page references in *italics* indicate photographs.

Anchovy(ies):
  -Garlic Mayonnaise, 40, *40*
  Parsley, and Garlic, Grilled Broccoli with, *18*, 19
Apple(s):
  Hard Cider–Braised Pork Shoulder, 172, *173*
  heirloom varieties, 168–69
  and Onions, Skillet, 174, *174*
  Summer, and Blackberry Pie, Monica's, 80–81, *81*
  White Sweet Potato Soup, 197
Asparagus:
  about, 32
  with Butter and Soy, 33
  Charcoal-Grilled, 34, *35*

Bacon:
  Choucroute Garnie 1-2-3, *246*, 247
  and Eggs in a Bag, Campfire, *28*, 29
  Smoked, and Vinegar, Turnip and Mustard Greens with, 220
  Smoked, Old-Fashioned Baked Beans with, *184*, 185
Beans:
  buying, 179
  field peas, about, 128–29
  Green, with Garlic Bread Crumbs and Tomatoes, *102*, 104
  Old-Fashioned Baked, with Smoked Bacon, *184*, 185
  Red Lentil Soup with Smoked Paprika, 191
  Roasted Pumpkin, and Ham Hocks, Macaroni with, 182–83, *183*
  Warm Edamame with Seven-Spice Powder, *132*, 133
  White, with Ham Hocks, Basic, 180–81
Beef:
  Basic Meat Stock, 177
  Grilled Grass-Fed Porterhouse with Crisp Herbs, *156*, 157
  Onion-Braised Overnight Brisket, 252
  Overnight Pot-on-Fire, 250, *251*
  Pot Roast with Gravy, *202*, 203–4
Beets, Curried, 248, *248*
Beets, Pickled, 142, *142*

Berry(ies):
  Monica's Blackberry and Summer Apple Pie, 80–81, *81*
  Pudding, Chilled, with Cream, 105, *105*
  Strawberry Ice Cream, 52, *52*
Beverages:
  The Homeward Angel, 88, *88*
  Michelada, 116, *116*
  Ruby Grapefruit Cordial, 213, *213*
  Tomato Juice, 116
Blackberry and Summer Apple Pie, Monica's, 80–81, *81*
Black Cod and Potatoes, Steamed, with Pounded Parsley, Garlic, and Mussels, 226, *227*
Black Drum, Pan-Roasted, 160, *161*
Black Sesame Sauce, 262–63
Bread Crumbs, Fine Lightly Toasted, 115
Broccoli:
  Grilled, with Parsley, Garlic, and Anchovies, *18*, 19
  serving ideas, 16
Brussels Sprout Leaves in Brown Butter, *161*, 163
Butter, homemade, preparing, 166–67

Cabbage:
  Choucroute Garnie 1-2-3, *246*, 247
  Green, Salad, 237, *238*
  Hot Slaw, 61
  Red, Sweet and Sour, Rye Bread, and Mustard, Crispy Chicken with, 228–29, *229*
  Sauerkraut, 143
  Savoy, Sautéed, with Speck and Lemon, 243, *243*
Cake, Juicy Satsuma Orange, 217–18, *218*
Carrot(s):
  and Fennel, Pickled, with Dill and Coriander, 138
  Glazed, *202*, 204
  Soup with Toasted Curry and Pistachios, 23–24, *24*
Catfish, Crispy Pan-Fried, with Hot Slaw, 60
Cauliflower
  Gratin with Aged Raw Milk Cheese, 17
  serving ideas, 16
Chard, Braised, with Fresh Hot Chiles, 151

Cheese:
  Aged Raw Milk, Cauliflower Gratin with, 17
  Blue, Red Grapefruit, and Sunflower Sprouts, Red Lettuces with, *194*, 195
  Broiled Baby Zucchini with Parmesan, 95
  Broiled Ripe Figs with Warm Ricotta and Honey, 134, *135*
  Kale Panini, *222*, 222–23
  Mexican Corn on the Cob, 93, *93*
  Warm Fresh Mozzarella with Grits, Grilled Radicchio, and Balsamic, 43, *45*
  Zucchini "Noodles" with Ricotta, 98
Cherry(ies):
  Cherry Stone Panna Cotta, 90
  The Homeward Angel, 88, *88*
  Sour, Pickled, *88*, 89
  Sweet, and Grilled Red Onion, Squab with, 86–87, *87*
Chestnuts:
  about, 210–11
  Roasted, in the Fireplace, 211
Chicken:
  Basic Meat Stock, 177
  Clay-Pot, in Fig Leaves, *192*, 193
  Crispy, with Rye Bread, Mustard, and Sweet and Sour Red Cabbage, 228–29, *229*
  Dark Poultry Stock, 177
  from Fickle Creek Farm, 36–37
  Fried, *102*, 103
  Hen and Dumplings, 38, 38–39
  Livers, Pan-Roasted, with Thyme and Schmaltz, 200
  No-Poach Poached, 257
  older breeds of, 100–101
  Roast, with Fennel and Spring Onions, 254–55
Chile(s):
  Fresh Hot, Braised Chard with, 151
  Hot Slaw, 61
  Jalapeño and Red Onion Escabeche, 237, *238*
  Oil, 141
  Peppers, Pickled, 141
  Red, and Crushed Fennel, Roasted Spareribs with, 258, *259*
  Salsa Roja, *238*, 239
  Salt-Cured, 140, *140*
Chocolate and Nuts, 158, *158*

Choucroute Garnie 1-2-3, *246*, 247
Cilantro:
  Hot Slaw, 61
  Salsa Roja, *238*, 239
  Salsa Verde, *238*, 239
Clams, Pan-Roasted, with Sake, 62
Colcannon with Scallion and Greens, 224
Collards, Baby, Wilted, with Ginger and
  Shoyu, *152*, 153
Corn:
  on the Cob, Mexican, 93, *93*
  Fritters, Crispy, 92, *92*
  and Potatoes, Spicy Crab and Shrimp
    Boil with, 84
  serving ideas, 91
Crab(s):
  and Garlic Fried Rice, 63
  and Shrimp Boil, Spicy, with Corn and
    Potatoes, 84
  soft-shell, about, 100–101
  Soft-Shell, Garlic and Black Pepper,
    122, 123
Crème Fraîche, 224
Cucumbers, Salted, 69, *69*
Cucumber Salad with Lemon Basil, *122*, 124
Curried Beets, 248, *248*
Curry, Toasted, and Pistachios, Carrot
  Soup with, 23–24, *24*
Curry Powder, 24
Custard, Honey Frozen, with Honeycomb
  Candy, 233–34, *234*

Dashi, 263
Desserts:
  Broiled Ripe Figs with Warm Ricotta
    and Honey, 134, *135*
  Cherry Stone Panna Cotta, 90
  Chilled Berry Pudding with Cream,
    105, *105*
  Chocolate and Nuts, 158, *158*
  Honey Frozen Custard with
    Honeycomb Candy, 233–34, *234*
  Juicy Satsuma Orange Cake, 217–18,
    218
  Monica's Blackberry and Summer
    Apple Pie, 80–81, *81*
  Rhubarb-Ginger Sorbet, 50
  Sour Cream Ice Cream with Sorghum,
    205
  Strawberry Ice Cream, 52, *52*
  Watermelon Jell-O with Gin, 126, *127*
Dressing, Escabeche, 240
Duck, Roast Moulard, with Kumquats
  and Salt-Cured Chiles, 214–16, *215*

Edamame, Warm, with Seven-Spice
  Powder, *132*, 133

Eggplant:
  Salad with Walnuts and Garlic, 107
  serving ideas, 106
Egg(s):
  Asparagus with Butter and Soy, 33
  and Bacon in a Bag, Campfire, *28*, 29
  from Fickle Creek Farm, 36–37
  Fried, and Black Sesame Sauce,
    Watercress with a, 262–63, *263*
  and Lemon, Escarole in Broth with, 178
Escabeche, Jalapeño and Red Onion,
  237, *238*
Escabeche Dressing, 240
Escarole in Broth with Lemon and Eggs,
  178

Fennel:
  and Carrots, Pickled, with Dill and
    Coriander, 138
  and Spring Onions, Roast Chicken
    with, 254–55
Fig Leaves, Clay-Pot Chicken in, *192*, 193
Figs:
  about, 132
  Pickled, Edith Calhoun's, 133
  Ripe, Broiled, with Warm Ricotta and
    Honey, 134, *135*
Fish. *See also* Anchovy(ies); Shellfish
  Cast-Iron-Skillet Fresh Trout with
    Cornmeal, 26
  Crispy Pan-Fried Catfish with Hot
    Slaw, 60
  Grilled Spanish Mackerel with Green
    Sauce, *56*, 57
  "junk" species, 159
  Pan-Roasted Black Drum, 160, *161*
  Steamed Black Cod and Potatoes
    with Pounded Parsley, Garlic, and
    Mussels, 226, *227*
  sustainable varieties, 54–55
  Whole, Baked in a Salt Crust, 165
Fritters, Crispy Corn, 92, *92*
Fruit. *See specific fruits*

Garlic:
  -Anchovy Mayonnaise, 40, *40*
  and Black Pepper Soft-Shell Crabs,
    122, 123
  Fried Rice and Crab, 63
  Green, and Lettuce, Fresh Peas with,
    53, *53*
  Oil, Roasted Shiitake Mushrooms
    with, 47
  Stewed, Slow-Cooked Black Kale with,
    221
Ginger:
  -Rhubarb Sorbet, 50

and Shoyu, Wilted Baby Collards with,
  152, 153
  Syrup, 50
Grains. *See also* Rice
  buying, 179
Grapefruit:
  Cordial, Ruby, 213, *213*
  Red, Blue Cheese, and Sunflower
    Sprouts, Red Lettuces with, *194*, 195
Green Beans with Garlic Bread Crumbs
  and Tomatoes, *102*, 104
Greens:
  Braised Chard with Fresh Hot Chiles,
    151
  Escarole in Broth with Lemon and
    Eggs, 178
  Fresh Peas with Lettuce and Green
    Garlic, 53, *53*
  Instant Spinach, 223
  Kale Panini, *222*, 222–23
  Pea, with Ume Plum Vinaigrette and
    Chive Blossoms, 48, *49*
  Red Lettuces with Blue Cheese, Red
    Grapefruit, and Sunflower Sprouts,
    194, 195
  and Scallion, Colcannon with, 224
  in Shrimp, Pea, and Rice Stew, 31
  Slow-Cooked Black Kale with Stewed
    Garlic, 221
  Spinach with Melted Leeks and
    Cardamom, 154
  Turnip and Mustard, with Smoked
    Bacon and Vinegar, 220
  Warm Fresh Mozzarella with Grits,
    Grilled Radicchio, and Balsamic,
    43, *45*
  watercress, growing, 260–61
  Watercress with a Fried Egg and Black
    Sesame Sauce, 262–63, *263*
  Wilted Baby Collards with Ginger and
    Shoyu, *152*, 153
  winter, about, 219–20

Ham:
  Hocks, Basic White Beans with,
    180–81
  Hocks, Beans, and Roasted Pumpkin,
    Macaroni with, 182–83, *183*
  from Ossabaw hogs, 20
  Roast Fresh, with Cracklings, 21–22,
    22
  Sautéed Savoy Cabbage with Speck and
    Lemon, 243, *243*
Herbs. *See also specific herbs*
  Crisp, Grilled Grass-Fed Porterhouse
    with, *156*, 157
  Green Sauce, *56*, 58

The Homeward Angel, 88, *88*
Honey:
    Frozen Custard with Honeycomb
        Candy, 233–34, *234*
    and Ricotta, Warm, Broiled Ripe Figs
        with, 134, *135*
    from Whitted Bowers Farm, 231–32

Ice Cream, Sour Cream, with Sorghum,
    205
Ice Cream, Strawberry, 52, *52*

Kale:
    Black, Slow-Cooked, with Stewed
        Garlic, 221
    Panini, *222*, 222–23
    serving ideas, 219–20
Kumquats and Salt-Cured Chiles, Roast
    Moulard Duck with, 214–16, *215*

Lemon verbena, about, 74
Lentil, Red, Soup with Smoked Paprika,
    191
Lettuce and Green Garlic, Fresh Peas
    with, 53, *53*
Lettuces, Red, with Blue Cheese, Red
    Grapefruit, and Sunflower Sprouts,
    194, 195
Livers, Chicken, Pan-Roasted, with
    Thyme and Schmaltz, 200

Macaroni with Beans, Roasted Pumpkin,
    and Ham Hocks, 182–83, *183*
Mackerel, Spanish, Grilled, with Green
    Sauce, 56, *57*
Mayonnaise, Garlic-Anchovy, 40, *40*
Meat. *See also* Beef; Pork
    Stock, Basic, 177
Melon:
    Salad, Spicy, with Peanuts and Mint,
        72, *73*
    Toasted Watermelon Seeds, 127
    Watermelon Jell-O with Gin, 126, *127*
Michelada, 116, *116*
Mint:
    Chile Oil, and Toasted Pine Nuts,
        Grilled Zucchini with, 96, *97*
    and Peanuts, Spicy Melon Salad with,
        72, *73*
Mushroom(s):
    shiitake, log-grown, 46
    Shiitake, Roasted, with Garlic Oil, 47
    Warm, Salad with Shallots and Sherry
        Vinegar, 198, *199*
Mussels, Pounded Parsley, and Garlic,
    Steamed Black Cod and Potatoes
    with, 226, *227*

Mustard and Turnip Greens with Smoked
    Bacon and Vinegar, 220
Mustard Sauce, 229

Nuts:
    Carrot Soup with Toasted Curry and
        Pistachios, 23–24, *24*
    chestnuts, about, 210–11
    and Chocolate, 158, *158*
    Eggplant Salad with Walnuts and
        Garlic, 107
    Pine, Toasted, Mint, and Chile Oil,
        Grilled Zucchini with, 96, *97*
    Roasted Chestnuts in the Fireplace, 211
    Spicy Melon Salad with Peanuts and
        Mint, *72*, 73

Oil, Chile, 141
Okra:
    Fried, with Indian Spices and Hot
        Tomato Relish, 108, *109*
    serving ideas, 106
Onion(s):
    and Apples, Skillet, 174, *174*
    -Braised Overnight Brisket, 252
    Red, and Jalapeño Escabeche, 237, *238*
    Red, Grilled, and Sweet Cherries,
        Squab with, 86–87, *87*
    Red, Preserves, *161*, 164
    Salted, 69
    salted, serving ideas, 70
    Spring, and Fennel, Roast Chicken
        with, 254–55
    Whole Roasted, 230
Orange, Juicy Satsuma, Cake, 217–18, *218*
Oyster(s):
    Raw, on Ice with Hot Sauce, 188, *189*
    shucking, 188
    Stew, 187

Panna Cotta, Cherry Stone, 90
Parsley:
    Green Sauce, 56, *58*
    Pounded, Garlic, and Mussels, Steamed
        Black Cod and Potatoes with, 226,
        227
Pasta. *See* Macaroni
Pea Greens:
    in Shrimp, Pea, and Rice Stew, 31
    with Ume Plum Vinaigrette and Chive
        Blossoms, 48, *49*
Peanuts and Mint, Spicy Melon Salad
    with, 72, *73*
Peas:
    field, about, 128–29
    Fresh, with Lettuce and Green Garlic,
        53, *53*

Shrimp, Pea, and Rice Stew, 31
Peppers. *See also* Chile(s):
    Marinated Roasted, in a Jar, 117
    serving ideas, 117
    Shishito, Flash-Fried, with Sea Salt,
        118, 119
Pickled Beets, 142, *142*
Pickled Carrots and Fennel with Dill and
    Coriander, 138
Pickled Chile Peppers, 141
Pickled Figs, Edith Calhoun's, 133
Pickled Green Tomatoes, *142*, 142–43
Pickled Pumpkin, 139
Pickled Sour Cherries, *88*, 89
Pie, Blackberry and Summer Apple,
    Monica's, 80–81, *81*
Pine Nuts, Toasted, Mint, and Chile Oil,
    Grilled Zucchini with, 96, *97*
Pistachios and Toasted Curry, Carrot
    Soup with, 23–24, *24*
Pork. *See also* Bacon; Ham:
    Basic Meat Stock, 177
    Choucroute Garnie 1-2-3, 246, *247*
    Miguel Torres's Carnitas, 236, *238*
    Roasted Spareribs with Crushed Fennel
        and Red Chiles, 258, *259*
    Shoulder, Hard Cider–Braised, 172,
        173
    Stock, Dark, 177
Potato(es). *See also* Sweet Potato(es):
    and Black Cod, Steamed, with
        Pounded Parsley, Garlic, and
        Mussels, 226, *227*
    Choucroute Garnie 1-2-3, 246, *247*
    Colcannon with Scallion and Greens,
        224
    and Corn, Spicy Crab and Shrimp Boil
        with, 84
    Salad, *56*, 59
Poultry. *See also* Chicken:
    Roast Moulard Duck with Kumquats
        and Salt-Cured Chiles, 214–16, *215*
    Squab with Grilled Red Onion and
        Sweet Cherries, 86–87, *87*
    Turkey Stock, 177
Preserves, Red Onion, *161*, 164
Pudding, Berry, Chilled, with Cream,
    105, *105*
Pumpkin:
    Pickled, 139
    Roasted, Beans, and Ham Hocks,
        Macaroni with, 182–83, *183*
    Smashed Candy Roaster, *161*, 162
Radicchio, Grilled, and Balsamic, Warm
    Fresh Mozzarella and Grits with,
    43, *45*
Ramps, about, 25

Ramps, Wilted, 27
Relish, Hot Tomato, 110
Rhubarb-Ginger Sorbet, 50
Rice:
    Garlic Fried, and Crab, 63
    and Shrimp, Pea Stew, 31
Rosemary and Black Pepper, Turnip Soup
        with, 242

Salads:
    Cucumber, with Lemon Basil, *122*, 124
    Eggplant, with Walnuts and Garlic, 107
    Green Cabbage, 237, *238*
    Hot Slaw, 61
    Melon, Spicy, with Peanuts and Mint,
        72, 73
    Pea Greens with Ume Plum Vinaigrette
        and Chive Blossoms, *48*, 49
    Potato, *56*, 59
    Red Lettuces with Blue Cheese, Red
        Grapefruit, and Sunflower Sprouts,
        194, 195
    "tomato tasting," creating, 70, *71*
    Warm Mushroom, with Shallots and
        Sherry Vinegar, 198, *199*
Salsa Roja, *238*, 239
Salsa Verde, *238*, 239
Salt Crust, Whole Fish Baked in a, 165
Salt-Cured Chiles, 140, *140*
Salted Cucumbers, 69, *69*
Salted Onions, 69
Salted Tomatoes, 70
Sandwiches:
    Kale Panini, *222*, 222–23
    Tomato, 112
Sauces:
    Black Sesame, 262–63
    Green, *56*, 58
    Mustard, 229
Sauerkraut:
    Choucroute Garnie 1-2-3, *246*, 247
    recipe for, 143
Sausages:
    Choucroute Garnie 1-2-3, *246*, 247
Scallion and Greens, Colcannon with,
        224
Seafood. *See* Fish; Shellfish
Seven-Spice Powder, 133
Shallots and Sherry Vinegar, Warm
        Mushroom Salad with, 198, *199*
Shellfish. *See also* Crab(s); Oyster(s);
        Shrimp:
    Pan-Roasted Clams with Sake, 62
    Steamed Black Cod and Potatoes
        with Pounded Parsley, Garlic, and
        Mussels, 226, *227*
    sustainable, about, 54–55

Shrimp:
    and Crab Boil, Spicy, with Corn and
        Potatoes, 84
    and Pea, Rice Stew, 31
    wild, flavor of, 30
Slaw, Hot, 61
Sorbet, Rhubarb-Ginger, 50
Soups. *See also* Stews:
    Carrot, with Toasted Curry and
        Pistachios, 23–24, *24*
    Red Lentil, with Smoked Paprika, 191
    Tomato, Cream of, with Tomato
        Leaves, 77
    Turnip, with Rosemary and Black
        Pepper, 242
    White Sweet Potato, 197
Sour Cream Ice Cream with Sorghum,
        205
Spanish Mackerel, Grilled, with Green
        Sauce, *56*, 57
Speck and Lemon, Sautéed Savoy
        Cabbage with, 243, *243*
Spices:
    Curry Powder, 24
    Seven-Spice Powder, 133
    Spice Cure, 216
Spinach, Instant, 223
Spinach with Melted Leeks and
        Cardamom, 154
Squab with Grilled Red Onion and Sweet
        Cherries, 86–87, *87*
Squash. *See also* Pumpkin; Zucchini:
    Slow-Cooked, with Butter and Basil,
        99, *99*
    Smashed Candy Roaster, *161*, 162
Stews:
    Hen and Dumplings, *38*, 38–39
    Oyster, 187
    Shrimp, Pea, and Rice, 31
Stock:
    Meat, Basic, 177
    Pork, Dark, 177
    Poultry, Dark, 177
    Turkey, 177
Strawberry Ice Cream, 52, *52*
Sunflower Sprouts, Blue Cheese, and Red
        Grapefruit, Red Lettuces with, *194*,
        195
Sweet Potato(es):
    about, 149
    White, Soup, 197
    Whole Roasted, with Butter, Molasses,
        and Salt, *148*, 149
Syrup, Ginger, 50

Tomatillos:
    Salsa Roja, *238*, 239

Salsa Verde, *238*, 239
Tomato(es):
    creating "tomato tasting" salad, 70, *71*
    and Garlic Bread Crumbs, Green Beans
        with, *102*, 104
    Green, Pickled, *142*, 142–43
    growing and harvesting, 111
    heirloom varieties, 111
    Juice, 116
    Michelada, 116, *116*
    Plum, Kathe's Baked, with Olive Oil
        and Bread Crumbs, 114, *115*
    Relish, Hot, 110
    Salted, 70
    Sandwich, 112
    Soup, Cream of, with Tomato Leaves,
        77
Trout, Fresh, Cast-Iron-Skillet, with
        Cornmeal, 26
Turkey Stock, 177
Turnip(s):
    about, 241
    Japanese, Roasted, with Honey, 244,
        245
    and Mustard Greens with Smoked
        Bacon and Vinegar, 220
    Soup with Rosemary and Black Pepper,
        242

Ume Plum Vinaigrette, 49

Vegetables. *See also specific vegetables*:
    Raw, with Garlic-Anchovy
        Mayonnaise, 40
    winter, about, 241
Vinaigrette, Ume Plum, 49

Walnuts and Garlic, Eggplant Salad with,
        107
Watercress:
    with a Fried Egg and Black Sesame
        Sauce, 262–63, *263*
    from Millarckee Farm, 260–61
Watermelon Jell-O with Gin, 126, *127*
Watermelon Seeds, Toasted, 127

Zucchini:
    Baby, Broiled, with Parmesan, 95
    Grilled, with Mint, Chile Oil, and
        Toasted Pine Nuts, 96, *97*
    "Noodles" with Ricotta, 98

ANDREA REUSING creates Asian flavors with local and seasonal ingredients at her acclaimed restaurant Lantern, one of *Gourmet*'s Top Fifty Restaurants. A James Beard Award nominee, she serves on the boards of the Center for Environmental Farming Systems and the Chefs Collaborative. Reusing lives in Chapel Hill with her husband and their two children. This is her first cookbook.